Theory
of
library
classification

OUTLINES OF MODERN LIBRARIANSHIP

Titles included in the series are

Children's librarianship
Local studies librarianship
Special librarianship
Book production
Library history
Current awareness services
Cataloguing
Music librarianship
History and theory of classification
Practical reference work
Public library administration
Medical librarianship

OUTLINES OF MODERN LIBRARIANSHIP

Theory
of
library
classification

by

BRIAN BUCHANAN

CLIVE BINGLEY LONDON

K G SAUR MUNICH · NEW YORK · PARIS

FIRST PUBLISHED 1979
SET IN 11 ON 12 POINT BASKERVILLE BY ALLSET
PRINTED AND BOUND IN THE UK BY
REDWOOD BURN LTD TROWBRIDGE AND ESHER
COPYRIGHT © 1979 BRIAN BUCHANAN
ALL RIGHTS RESERVED
ISBN: 0-85157-270-7

CLIVE BINGLEY LTD
COMMONWEALTH HOUSE
1-19 NEW OXFORD STREET, LONDON WC1

K G SAUR VERLAG
P O BOX 71 10 09, D-8000 MUNICH 71

K G SAUR PUBLISHING INC
175 FIFTH AVENUE, NEW YORK NY 10010

K G SAUR EDITEUR
38 RUE DE BASSANO, F-75008 PARIS

British Library Cataloguing in Publication Data

Buchanan, Brian
   Theory of library classification. — (Outlines
   of modern librarianship; vol. 11).
   1. Classification — Books
   I. Title   II. Series
   025.4   Z696.A4

   ISBN 0-85157-270-7

CONTENTS

	Introduction	7
1	Classification: definition and uses	9
2	The relationships between classes	17
3	Enumerative and faceted schemes	27
4	Decisions	37
5	The construction of a faceted scheme: I	45
6	The construction of a faceted scheme: II	59
7	Notation: I	71
8	Notation: II	81
9	Notation: III	95
10	The alphabetical subject index	101
11	General classification schemes	105
12	Objections to systematic order	119
13	Automatic classification	123
	Index	135

For my parents

Jerry laughed. 'He's always seeing patterns. There aren't any. Not really. The disordered mind sees order everywhere—systems take shape from the movement of the wind in the leaves of the trees—patterns merge as the mad eye selects only what it wishes to see. Patterns are madness, for the most part.' — Michael Moorcock: *The condition of muzak*

INTRODUCTION

THERE are two kinds of outline. One attempts to cover all the topics in a field of study at a more-or-less equally superficial level; the second selects certain areas for discussion, in the hope that they provide a structure for the study of the subject, and that the discussion is detailed enough to ensure that these key areas are sufficiently understood as a sure basis for further study. This outline of library classification is of the second type; it follows that some topics usually found in elementary textbooks on this subject are deliberately omitted. The book is based on the content of the classification sections of the two-year core course in indexing given at the School of Librarianship, Loughborough Technical College, and I must thank my colleagues and students (both past and present in both categories) for the help—sometimes given unwittingly—without which it could not have been written.

The abbreviations for particular schemes discussed in the text are: BC = Bibliographic Classification; CC = Colon Classification; CLIS = Classification of Library and Information Science; LC = Library of Congress Classification; LEC = London Education Classification; SC = Subject Classification; and UDC = Universal Decimal Classification. Numerals indicate editions. The following typographical conventions have been followed: document titles are given in italics; names of subjects are given initial capitals; and the names of classes are fully capitalised, except where shown as part of a schedule.

Most examples in this book have been drawn from Zoology, and the model schemes are on the same subject (incidentally they are not model schemes on Zoology; they are models of the techniques under discussion). The reason for this is that most people know the meaning of zoological terms, and, more important, are aware of the relationships between different classes in this discipline—for example, that butterflies are a kind of insect, and that insects are a kind of invertebrate. The importance of this was brought home to me during the week in which this introduction was typed (the last part of the book to be completed, of course). I set my first-year students an exercise on DC18, which was intended to demonstrate, among other things, the scheme's failure in specificity. One of the works to be classified was called *Perpendicular church buildings*. Some students did not know that this was a style of architecture, and one very ingeniously gave it the notation for the class CHURCH TOWERS, on the grounds that these are perpendicular parts of churches! This is less likely to happen with titles such as *The respiration of owls*.

BB
January 1979

ONE

CLASSIFICATION: DEFINITION AND USES

CLASSIFICATION is the act of grouping like things together. All the members of a group—or class—produced by classification share at least one characteristic which members of other classes do not possess. The 'things' which are classified may be concrete entities, the ideas of such entities, or abstractions. For example, we could house lions, tigers and leopards close to each other in a zoo—grouping them because we perceive that they share a characteristic (we could call it 'catness') which elephants, sea-lions and spiders do not possess. Suppose, though, that zoos did not exist, so that we could not group the actual, concrete animals: we could still appreciate the relationship between the idea of the lion, the idea of the tiger and the idea of the leopard, and group them in our minds. Similarly, we could group abstractions—properties of things, and operations and activities performed by things or on things.

The recognition of likenesses may be performed by machines or by human beings. Human perception of shared characteristics may be intuitive (for example, quite young children can tell that both St Bernards and Yorkshire terriers belong to the same class, and are able to assign a kind of dog new to them to the same class—but they would not be able to state the characteristics which these animals share, any more than most adults could); or it may be the result of conscious thought.

Classification displays the relationships between things, and between classes of things. We see that members of the class PAINTINGS differ from members of the class DRAWINGS; but also that these two classes have a closer relationship with each other than either has with the class SCULPTURE, because they share the quality of being two-dimensional. In the same way we appreciate that these three classes are related, because they are all kinds of what is called Fine art—distinct from performing arts such as Music. The result of classification is the display of a network or pattern of relationships. We use this pattern for many purposes, in some cases unconsciously—by intuition—in others consciously.

Through classification we cope with the multitude of unorganised impressions we receive by way of our senses; we can use the pattern to impose order on chaos, 'placing' what we see, hear, feel, smell and taste, within it. Classification simplifies the process of thought, because there are, naturally, far fewer classes than there are members of classes. It enables us to generalise, and, as Jevons says(1) 'all thought, all reasoning, so far as it deals with general names or general notions, may be said to consist in classification.'

This is most obviously true in formal thinking or logic, which is concerned with kinds of statements, types of arguments and classes of things—Jevons goes on to suggest that 'it would hardly be too much to define logic as the theory of classification'. When we define a thing we make use of classification, for 'a definition consists primarily of two parts, the proximate genus and the specific difference of the concept defined.'(2) That is, in defining we refer to the class which contains the thing to be defined, and then we state the characteristic which differentiates the thing from other members of the same class—as in 'a rifle is a firearm with a spirally grooved bore'.

We design courses of study, guided by classification—as Aristotle did(3); and when we pursue research we make use of classification as a kind of map of knowledge. In society we perceive classes (which is hardly surprising, seeing that 'class' is derived from 'clasis'—the calling together of Roman citizens in groups according to degree of wealth); and our pattern of relationships may be extended to cover the whole universe and time, justifying and giving meaning to human society:

'The Sioux were a systematic people. They were organizers and classifiers. As the universe was intricately patterned into hierarchies and divisions, so was the nation.'(4)

At the mundane level, classification has everyday practical uses: supermarkets are organised so that all products of the same type are together—meat, vegetables, dairy produce— each further subdivided (butter, margarine, cooking fats, milk, cream): without classification, supermarkets would be even more unpleasant to use than they are with it. Warehouses and factory stores arrange goods and parts together according to how they are used. Schoolchildren are streamed. Record shops group gramophone records—or at least their covers; and, of course, libraries classify documents.

Classification and indexing
The examples above show how pervasive and fundamental classification is as a tool. In this book we are going to examine one of its uses only—as a tool in the organisation of stores of documents.

A document is the physical carrier of a message. A book is a document; so is a gramophone record; so are films, slides, periodicals, cards bearing the names and addresses of local organisations in a reference library's files, and machine-readable media. The messages they bear may be simple facts, or views on and interpretations of events, or works of art— *Hamlet* is a message, just as the *Jupiter* symphony is, or as my telephone number recorded in a directory is. When the number of documents becomes too great for a person seeking a particular message to scan through them all it becomes necessary to organise them; when this task becomes too great to be performed informally it is institutionalised—that is, specialists are appointed to carry out the task. These specialists are librarians and other information workers, whose function it is to mediate between their clients and the documents containing the messages they need.

We can state the librarian's contribution to society more precisely: he enables clients to find any required subset of documents from the total set as quickly and easily as possible. To do this he selects and collects documents; organises his collection; cooperates with other librarians and information workers; and helps and encourages his clients to use documents. The central task, on which the others depend, is the organisation of the collection—the arrangement of the documents in some helpful order, and the provision of catalogues

11

and indexes which act as both keys and complements to that order. We call the techniques developed to bring about this organisation 'indexing'.

As indexing is concerned with the easy location of sub-sets—that is, of classes—of documents, it is clear that all indexing techniques are applications of classification. The characteristics which define the various classes sought by a client differ: they include the name of an author, the name of a series of works (eg *New naturalist series*), the name of a translator, illustrator, composer, performer or film director; and the name of the subject about which messages are required. However, in this book we will consider only classification by subject (or in some cases by form of document); we shall limit our topic further by not considering subject indexing techniques other than those which use concept indexing; and within that limitation we shall be concerned for the most part with the classification scheme, which is a tool for the production of systematic order. This last, narrowest, meaning is the one generally understood when the term ' classification' in indexing is used, and it is in this sense that we shall use it for the rest of this book.

Concept indexing
Concepts are the ideas of things, to be distinguished from the names of things. The same concept may have many names (in different languages—book, Buch, livre, libro; or in the same language, synonyms—firearms/guns, adolescents/teen-agers, panthers/leopards); a name may stand for many different concepts—that is, it may be a homonym (alienation/alienation/alienation/alienation; bridge/bridge/bridge); and some concepts may not have their own names (for example, a pony is a horse which is not more than fourteen hands high; what is the name for a horse which stands more than four-teen hands high?) In concept indexing, the indexer re-cognises the concepts with which a document deals, rather than merely accepting the names he finds in the document. In practice, this means that he provides means for a client to find all works on a concept no matter what name the client uses for the concept, nor what name is used for the concept in the document; and that he distinguishes the different

12

meanings of a homonym, so that the client is not led to irrelevant documents by the indexing system. If we call the set of names or symbols which represent classes of documents 'the index vocabulary', then we can say that in concept indexing the index vocabulary is controlled, because the indexer has controlled synonyms and homonyms. Failure to control the index vocabulary (seen in 'natural language' systems, which merely use the names of concepts found in the documents) may lead to the failure to find material on a subject which is, in fact, available in a collection; or to the irritation of being presented with irrelevant documents.

Controlled vocabularies are usually also structured; that is, they display the relationships between different concepts, either by means of references:

Insects *see also* Bees

or by keeping works on related subjects close to each other, through systematic order. Structured vocabularies make it easier for the client to broaden, narrow and extend his search, so that he retrieves more documents in his search, or retrieves fewer irrelevant ones. A classification scheme is an example of a controlled and structured index vocabulary.

Systematic order

Systematic order between documents (or between records of documents in a catalogue) is an order which of itself displays the relationships between the subjects of documents; it collocates, or keeps together, works on the same subject, and juxtaposes these with closely related works. This sequence illustrates the principle: vertebrates—fish—birds—mammals—rodents—rats—mice—insectivores—hedgehogs.

Here we see the class RATS, kept with its closely related class MICE; these are preceded by the class which contains them, RODENTS, and followed by INSECTIVORES, which is related to the class RODENTS; INSECTIVORES is in turn followed by the classes it contains, such as HEDGEHOGS. Systematic order is, as we have said, one method of displaying structure; and so it brings the advantages of a structured vocabulary with the additional facility of easy browsing through the sequence. Systematic order is the peculiar contribution of the classification scheme to indexing.

Uses of systematic order

The most obvious application of systematic order is the placing of books in order on the shelves of libraries—this is what most people think of as 'classification'. This use enables clients to browse for themselves among the stock, giving them greater autonomy, and making open-access libraries possible (or at least efficient—we can imagine an open-access library with stock not in systematic order, but it is difficult to see how it would be used).

Systematic order is used in the classified catalogue, obviously; but a classification scheme can also provide the basis for the display of structure in an alphabetical subject catalogue—the references:

Vertebrates *see also* Mammals
Mammals *see also* Rodents
Rodents *see also* Rats
Mice *see also* Rats

could be easily derived from the systematic sequence above.

A classification scheme can, in fact, form the basis of any kind of controlled and structured vocabulary: alphabetical subject indexes to classified catalogues may be derived from the classification scheme in use, by the technique of chain indexing; thesauri for post-coordinate indexes are often produced from classification schemes, and attempts have been made to use the notation from schemes—that is, the codes which represent classes, usually found on the spines of books in classified libraries—directly as index vocabularies in post-coordinate systems(5). Finally, systematic order may be used for records of documents on machine-readable media, to save time in computer searches; and to make the broadening and narrowing of searches through the computer easier.

Classification, then, is about the discovery and the display of relationships; in our narrow sense the display is to be by means of systematic order. Let's begin our exploration of this technique by considering the kinds of relationship which classification schemes are called on to display.

REFERENCES

1 Jevons, W Stanley *Elementary lessons in logic* Macmillan, 1870.

2 Bowen, Francis *Treatise on logic* 2nd ed, Cambridge (Mass), Sever & Francis, 1864.

3 see, for example, Burnett, J *Aristotle on education* Cambridge University Press, 1926.

4 Hassrick, Royal B *The Sioux* Norman, University of Oklahoma Press, 1964.

5 for a brief account of some applications of a particular scheme, see Foskett, A C *The Universal Decimal Classification* Bingley, 1973.

TWO

THE RELATIONSHIPS BETWEEN CLASSES

THE relationships which our classification scheme must be able to express are of two kinds. The first of these is the relationship between classes which occur together in statements which represent the subjects of documents—for example, that between 'play', 'development' and 'primates' in the subject statement The Role of Play in the Development of Primates. Our scheme will not be efficient unless it enables us to specify this subject precisely and unambiguously: if it does not allow us to include all the elements, or if it fails to distingush between, say, 'the development of play in primates' and 'play in the development of primates', then our clients may be forced to examine many irrelevant documents before they find the information they are looking for.

The second kind of relationship is that which exists between different subject statements. The subject statement 'The Behaviour of Apes' explicitly states a relationship of the first kind, but it also has an unstated—an implicit—relationship with our first document's subject: apes are a kind of primate, and play is a kind of behaviour. Because of this, both documents could be useful to a client looking for information on either's subject; if our classification scheme does not display the relationship, then the client may overlook valuable material.

We could call the first kind of relationship 'syntactical' because it involves a grammatical connection between classes (shown on the verbal plane by verbs, prepositions and wordforms), and the second kind 'hierarchical', because it involves the recognition of subordination, such as that between a thing and its kinds (eg primates—apes), a thing and its processes (eg birds—respiration of birds) and a thing and its parts (eg haddocks—haddocks' eyes).

17

Syntactical relationships

If we include 'no relationship' then there are four kinds of syntactical relationship, which means that our scheme must provide for four kinds of classes. These conveniently fall into two groups of two:

Classes resulting from syntactical relationships

Simple classes		Composite classes	
Elemental classes	Superimposed classes	Complex classes	Compound classes

Simple classes are those in which the relationship merely defines one kind of thing. Elemental classes are those in which that thing is defined by only one characteristic—they are classes containing no syntactical relationships, but are the elements from which classes with such relationships are built up. Classes such as RESPIRATION (a physiological process), PRIMATES (a kind of animal), FORESTS (a kind of habitat), ANIMALS OF THE SEA SHORE (a kind of animal defined by where it lives) and HIBERNATING ANIMALS (a kind of animal defined by habit) are examples of elemental classes.

Superimposed classes (the term is taken from Ranganathan (1)) are simple classes defined by more than one characteristic; for example, the class TROPICAL FORESTS is a kind of habitat defined by latitude and by type of ground cover; MARINE MAMMALS is a kind of animal defined by both habitat and by zoologists' taxonomy; BRITISH MIGRATORY BIRDS is a kind of animal defined by place where it can be found, by habit and by zoologists' taxonomy. Because superimposed classes are like compound classes, in that they both contain more than one elemental class, it is possible to mistake one for the other, as is done in an otherwise excellent textbook in our field. Unless the distinction is maintained it is not possible to differentiate between, say, the superimposed class MIGRATORY BIRDS and the compound class THE MIGRATION OF BIRDS; or between the superimposed class TIMBER KAYAKS and the compound class TIMBER FOR KAYAKS. The distinction is not always necessary, but the possibility must be recognised. A former colleague,

18

David Hope, suggested a test to distinguish the two kinds of classes: if it is possible to insert the words 'which are also' between the elemental classes then the class is a superimposed class; for example, 'British animals which are also migratory animals which are also birds'.

In a composite class, different kinds of things are in a relationship of interaction; the relationship does not define a kind of thing. Compare the two classes WOODLAND BIRDS and THE RESPIRATION OF BIRDS; in the first case, each elemental class is made a kind of the other by the relationship—woodland birds are a kind of bird, and also a kind of woodland animal; in the second case, however, the relationship does not make the elemental class BIRDS a kind of the elemental class RESPIRATION, nor the class RESPIRATION a kind of bird.

Both complex and compound classes deal with relationships between more than one kind of thing; the difference between them is in the extent to which these components retain their identities in the relationship. In a complex class, the interaction between the component classes leaves them still separable, in that their contributions to the whole remain distinct; in a compound class the components fuse, and cannot be separated out. As has been said before(2) the distinction is similar to that between a mixture and a compound in chemistry. A mixture of iron filings and salt remains iron filings and salt despite the mixing, and the elements can be separated mechanically (eg by dissolving the salt or by extracting the iron filings with a magnet); but a compound of oxygen and hydrogen is water, a new substance quite different from its component elements—for example, water is liquid under normal temperature and pressure, while both its components are gases.

Ranganathan underlines this difference between the two kinds of composite class by calling complex classes 'loose assemblages'(3). His name for the components of such a class is 'phases', and he calls their relationship a 'phase relationship'. The phases of a complex class may be elemental, superimposed or compound classes, and they are linked on the verbal plane by terms which specify the nature of their relationship. Examples of phase relationships are Comparison

19

(eg A COMPARISON BETWEEN MIGRATORY AND HIBERNATING ANIMALS—an example whose phases are elemental classes; and THE RESPIRATION OF BATS COMPARED WITH THE RESPIRATION OF BIRDS—an example whose phases are compound classes); Influence (eg THE INFLUENCE OF DARWINISM ON CHRISTIAN THOUGHT); and Exposition (eg AN ETHOLOGICAL EXPLANATION OF AGGRESSION IN MAN, in which the subject—man's aggression—is expounded from a particular viewpoint). In all these cases the documents will give information on both phases, as well as on their relationship—the elements remain distinguishable.

The other commonly cited phase relationship is Bias (eg STATISTICS FOR BIOLOGISTS) in which information about one specialism is presented in terms suitable for practitioners in another; but it seems likely that this is not a true phase relationship (there will be little or no information about biology in the document from which our subject statement was taken, for example), and it might be better to treat such classes as a subject presented in a certain form rather than as a complex class. This is done in UDC, which uses the notation (024) from its Form of presentation facet to represent 'books for special type of user'.

If we compare one of our complex class examples—say, A COMPARISON BETWEEN MIGRATORY AND HIBERNATING ANIMALS—with a compound class, such as THE INTELLIGENCE OF RATS, we can see what is meant by the fusion of components in this last kind of class. The document from which the compound class statement was derived does not give information about intelligence in general and information about rats in general, and then bring the two subjects into a relationship, in the way in which the complex class gives information about migratory animals and information about hibernating animals and then compares the two; instead, it deals with only one aspect of the rat, and with intelligence in one kind of animal—each of the elemental classes modifies the other, and in the resulting compound they are indissolubly merged.

Some documents give information on more than one kind of thing without dealing with a relationship between them.

20

An example is a work entitled *Reptiles and amphibians*, in which part of the work gives information on one subject and part gives information on the other. We might call documents of this kind 'polytopical works'. The subjects of polytopical works do not form a new kind of class and, for classification purposes, either each distinct subject should be treated as though it constituted a separate work (eg, in an alphabetical catalogue there could be two entries for our example, one under the name REPTILES, the other under the name AMPHIBIANS) or, when the subjects contained in the work exhaust a more general class then that class should be used to represent the document's subject (eg a work entitled *Frogs, toads, newts and salamanders* should have AMPHIBIANS as its subject statement).

Hierarchical relationships
Hierarchical relationships are based upon the principle of subordination or inclusion. If one class wholly includes another, or if two classes are wholly included by a third, then the pair has a significant relationship which our scheme must display. For example, the class BUTTERFLIES is wholly contained by the class LEPIDOPTERA—butterflies are a kind of lepidoptera.

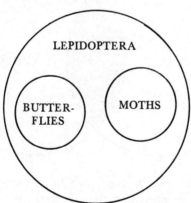

Our client looking for information on lepidoptera must be led to works on butterflies as well, because butterflies are lepidoptera; the client looking for information on butterflies will find information contained in works on lepidoptera useful for the same reason. Similarly, the relationship between the classes BUTTERFLIES and MOTHS must be shown by our scheme, because both are included by the class LEPIDOPTERA; the client looking for lepidoptera will want to find documents on butterflies and on moths, as well as general works on lepidoptera; the client looking for information on moths may want to broaden his search to include general works on lepidoptera, and extend it to include works on the closely related class BUTTERFLIES.

The kind of hierarchical relationship discussed so far is called generic—that between a thing and its kinds: between a genus and its species. This is an absolute relationship, which does not depend on the existence of documents on the related subjects (although, of course, if no documents were ever produced on the related subjects this absolute relationship would be of no interest to us as classificationists). The generic relationship is not the only kind of hierarchical relationship, however. Consider the subject statement, Play in Primates.

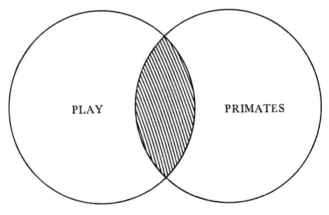

The class is quite clearly contained by the classes PLAY and PRIMATES: it is narrower than either. It is not, though, about a *kind* of play, nor about a *kind* of primate—the relationship between it and its parent classes is not a generic one, and only exists because an author has produced a work involving it: it is not a 'natural' or absolute relationship.

Still, we must display this broader-narrower relationship—between a thing and its activities—for the same reasons that we must display generic relationships. Similar relationships are those between a thing and operations on it (eg RES-PIRATION—EXPERIMENTS ON RESPIRATION); between a thing and its parts (eg INSECTS—INTEGUMENT OF INSECTS); and a thing and its properties (eg RATS—INTEL-LIGENCE OF RATS).

Broader-narrower relationships between more complicated subject statements may be difficult to perceive. The rule is that if one or more components of one subject statement are broader than the corresponding components of another, and the remaining components are the same, then the first class is broader than the second; eg EXPERIMENTS ON THE BEHAVIOUR OF PRIMATES is broader than EXPERI-MENTS ON THE BEHAVIOUR OF APES

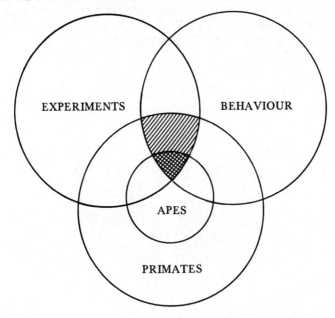

and broader than EXPERIMENTS ON THE PLAY OF PRIMATES. (Of course THE BEHAVIOUR OF PRIMATES is broader than any of these). In some cases, different components 'cancel out'; for example, PLAY IN PRIMATES

23

cannot be said to be either broader or narrower than BE-
HAVIOUR OF APES.

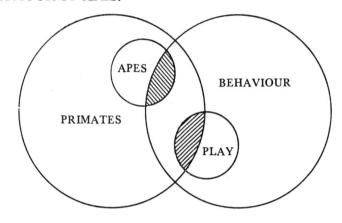

Again, in some cases it is not possible for one class to include
another—for example, PLAY IN BEARS is neither broader
nor narrower than PLAY IN PRIMATES.

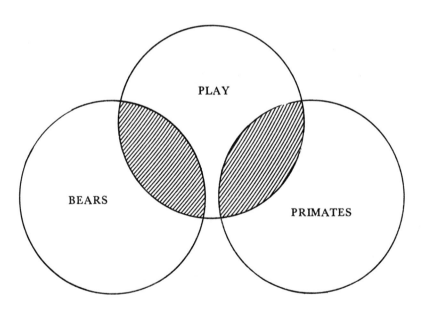

When we discuss hierarchical relationships we can make use of the following terminology: a class which contains another is said to be superordinate to that class; the contained class is said to be subordinate to the containing classes; classes which are neither broader nor narrower than each other, and which share the same immediate superordinate class, are said to be coordinate; and classes which are neither broader nor narrower than each other while not sharing the same immediate superordinate class, although in the same hierarchy, are said to be collateral. For example, in the following diagram of a hierarchy the class VERTEBRATES is subordinate to ANIMALS, superordinate to each of the classes FISH, AMPHIBIANS, REPTILES, BIRDS and MAMMALS, and coordinate with the class INVERTEBRATES. The classes FISH, AMPHIBIANS, REPTILES, BIRDS and MAMMALS are coordinate with each other, collateral with the classes WORMS, ARACHNIDS and INSECTS, and subordinate to the class VERTEBRATES.

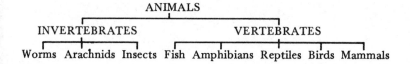

REFERENCES

1 Ranganathan, S R *The Colon Classification* New Brunswick, Rutgers University Graduate School of Library Service, 1965.
It is worth noting that although the terminology used in this present book is derived from that of Dr Ranganathan, some terms have been given a different meaning—especially Composite and Compound classes, in this chapter.
2 This analogy seems so obvious, and has been with me so long, that I assumed that I had found it in the literature. If I did, I cannot find it now, and none of my colleagues remembers seeing it. Unless somebody else can supply a source, I shall claim it as my own invention.
3 Ranganathan, S R *Prolegomena to library classification* 3rd ed, Bombay; London, Asia Publishing House, 1967.

THREE

ENUMERATIVE AND FACETED SCHEMES

WE CAN arrange for our scheme to express the different kinds of relationships discussed in the previous chapter in two ways. The traditional method is to postulate a universe of knowledge (all knowledge in the case of a general scheme, some part of it—eg Social welfare, Librarianship, Diamond technology—in the case of a special scheme) and to divide this into successively narrower classes, which will include all the elemental, superimposed and compound classes which the scheme may have to accommodate, arranged in an order displaying their hierarchical relationships. Classification schemes of this kind are called 'enumerative', because they enumerate, or list, all the required classes (except complex classes—it is not possible to predict the phase relationships which authors may perceive: the name 'author attributed relationships' sometimes given to them indicates their idiosyncratic nature, and usually the attempt to list them is not made). The *Decimal classification* is an obvious example of an enumerative scheme—its very name shows that it divides the whole of knowledge into ten main classes, and each of these into ten principal sub-classes, and each of these sub-classes into ten, and so on as far as is necessary (although it is worth noting that the decimal principle is more apparent than real).

The second method relies not on the breakdown of a universe, but on building up from particular documents' subject statements. By this method, subject statements are analysed into their component elemental classes, and it is these classes only which are listed in the scheme; and their generic relationships are the only relationships displayed on its pages. When the classifier using such a scheme has to

27

express a superimposed, complex or compound class, he does so by assembling its elemental classes—in practice, by joining their notations together, a process known as 'synthesis'. We usually refer to such schemes as 'faceted', because their elemental classes are arranged in groups called facets; but an alternative name, 'analytico-synthetic', is more revealing of their nature—although a more clumsy term.(1)

The following examples illustrate the differences between faceted and enumerative schemes. They are obviously demonstration models—no real scheme would be compiled containing only nine classes, as does the faceted example. The reason why so few classes are included that the schemes are obviously unrealistic will soon be clear. First, the faceted scheme:

(processes facet)
    Physiology
        Respiration
        Reproduction

(animals facet)
    (by habitat subfacet)
        Water animals
        Land animals
    (by zoologists' taxonomy subfacet)
        Invertebrates
            Insects
        Vertebrates
            Reptiles

Now, the enumerative scheme:

Physiology
    Respiration
    Reproduction

Water animals
    Physiology of water animals
        Respiration of water animals
        Reproduction of water animals

Land animals
　Physiology of land animals
　　Respiration of land animals
　　Reproduction of land animals

Invertebrates
　Physiology of invertebrates
　　Respiration of invertebrates
　　Reproduction of invertebrates
　Water invertebrates
　　Physiology of water invertebrates
　　　Respiration of water invertebrates
　　　Reproduction of water invertebrates
　Land invertebrates
　　Physiology of land invertebrates
　　　Respiration of land invertebrates
　　　Reproduction of land invertebrates

　Insects
　　Physiology of insects
　　　Respiration of insects
　　　Reproduction of insects
　　Water insects
　　　Physiology of water insects
　　　　Respiration of water insects
　　　　Reproduction of water insects
　　Land insects
　　　Physiology of land insects
　　　　Respiration of land insects
　　　　Reproduction of land insects

Vertebrates
　Physiology of vertebrates
　　Respiration of vertebrates
　　Reproduction of vertebrates
　Water vertebrates
　　Physiology of water vertebrates
　　　Respiration of water vertebrates
　　　Reproduction of water vertebrates
　Land vertebrates
　　Physiology of land vertebrates
　　　Respiration of land vertebrates
　　　Reproduction of land vertebrates

Reptiles
    Physiology of reptiles
        Respiration of reptiles
        Reproduction of reptiles
    Water reptiles
        Physiology of water reptiles
            Respiration of water reptiles
            Reproduction of water reptiles
    Land reptiles
        Physiology of land reptiles
            Respiration of land reptiles
            Reproduction of land reptiles

Now, remember that although the faceted scheme includes only elemental classes, while the enumerative also contains superimposed classes such as LAND INSECTS and compound classes such as RESPIRATION OF REPTILES, both schemes can be used to express precisely the same number of classes; the difference is that in the enumerative scheme classes with more than one elemental component are listed ready-made, while with the faceted scheme the classifier will have to make his own multi-element classes by synthesis. With this in mind, we can appreciate how much more time-consuming, complicated and tedious the construction of an enumerative scheme is, compared with that of a faceted scheme; and also how much more bulky the result will be (in the third abridged English edition of UDC the class Literature—a completely faceted class in this scheme—takes up one page; in DC18 the same class occupies forty pages). This, of course, is why our examples were so unrealistically small scale.

This difference between the two kinds of schemes affects only compilers; unfortunately, other problems associated with enumerative schemes give them a tendency to inefficiency. They are not normally compiled with the rigour and care shown in our small scale example above; the size and complexity of the operation lead compilers to omit classes which they think are not needed, or simply to forget to provide them. This is especially true of classes with more than one element. Of course, if you do not attempt to list superimposed or compound classes (that is, if you are compiling a faceted scheme) then you cannot omit any; but if you try to include them all, it is likely that you will forget or ignore some; and it will not be possible for the users of your scheme to express them when necessary. DC18 provides many examples of this; consider these selections from the class Education:

372	Elementary education
372.1	The elementary school
372.10421	Public (elementary schools)
372.6	Language arts (in the elementary school)
372.61	Grammar and word study (in the elementary school)
372.632	Spelling (in the elementary school)
373	Secondary education
373.1	The secondary school
373.19	Curriculum (in secondary schools) (but this does not include 'specific subjects'; these must go in 375)
374	Adult education
375	Curriculums (in education other than elementary)
375.42152	Spelling
378	Higher education

With this enumerative scheme we can express those classes listed—elemental classes, such as SECONDARY SCHOOLS; superimposed classes, such as PUBLIC ELEMENTARY SCHOOLS (a kind of school defined by level and by ownership); and compound classes, such as THE SECONDARY SCHOOL CURRICULUM; but we cannot express others which the compilers have left out, either by design or by accident. For example, we cannot express the combination of any particular curriculum subject with the class SECONDARY SCHOOLS, although many books are written on this kind of topic; eg, although the class SPELLING IN ELEMENTARY EDUCATION is there, the class SPELLING IN SECONDARY EDUCATION is not. More surprisingly, we cannot even express the elemental class SPELLING (in education), because there are two places for it, each in an enumerated compound class—SPELLING IN ELEMENTARY

31

EDUCATION and SPELLING IN EDUCATION AT LEVELS OTHER THAN ELEMENTARY; and this is true of all other curriculum subjects.

Now compare this with a faceted scheme, BC2:

(curriculum facet)
JKG Mother tongue
JKG Y Reading and writing
JKH   Reading
JKJ   Writing
JKJ M   Spelling

(educand facet)
J LH Pre-school education
JM Primary, elementary education
JN Secondary education

With elemental classes such as these in a faceted scheme, we can express anything available in DC18, but in addition we have those classes not provided for by that scheme—eg the elemental class SPELLING and, through synthesis, the compound class SPELLING IN SECONDARY EDUCATION:

SECONDARY EDUCATION	JN
+ SPELLING	JKJ M
SPELLING IN SECONDARY EDUCATION	JN KJM

(We have omitted the redundant initial J from JKJ M in synthesising, because it simply means Education and is already present in JN; and we had better say that BC2 prefers to present its notation in groups of three digits starting from the left, so that the final notation would actually be written JNK JM.)

One of the oddities of DC in its modern editions has been its failure to provide for an elemental class, while providing for its elemental subdivisions; for example, in the current edition the class NINETEENTH CENTURY ARCHITEC-TURE cannot be expressed, although particular manifest-ations in that period (eg Classical revival, Gothic revival) are enumerated, and so is the class EARLY MODERN ARCHI-TECHTURE 1400-1800. What is peculiarly odd is that the

32

compilers recognise the class, but instruct the classifier to place works on it in the general number for MODERN ARCHITECTURE, 1400-; so that one could find the following unhelpful sequence of books on the shelves of an architectural library misguided enough to use the scheme:

724	Modern architecture, 1400-
724	Nineteenth century architecture
724.1	Early modern architecture, 1400-1800
724.19	Baroque, rococo
724.2	Classical revival
724.3	Gothic revival

etc.

The nineteenth century architecture example illustrates the point that order in enumerative schemes is sometimes unhelpful, as well as that it may not be possible to specify classes. The failure to give a helpful order may be due to errors arising from the complexity of compilation, but many have a wilful air about them, as though the compilers wanted to obstruct library clients rather than help them. DC18 is a culprit here too (we no longer subscribe to the conspiracy theory—that a heavily-disguised member of the LC classification office has infiltrated the DC office, and is engaged in sabotage—but now accept that some DC staff do not appreciate the functions of a classification scheme; and we do not start with an anti-DC bias: DC examples are chosen because they are spectacular, and the scheme is popular and accessible, so that you can easily check the statements we make about it). Consider the following sequence of classes, from Music:

788	Wind instruments
788.01	Brass instruments
788.05	Woodwind instruments
788.056	Reed instruments
788.1	Trumpets
788.2	Trombones
788.4	Horns
788.5	Flutes
788.6	Single-reed instruments
788.62	Clarinets

| 788.7 | Oboes |
| 788.8 | Bassoons |

We have not yet discussed the principles of helpful order, yet it should be clear that the above order is very unhelpful: to separate works on brass instruments in general from works on particular brass instruments (such as trumpets) by works on woodwind instruments; to separate works on single-reed instruments from those on reed instruments in general by works which are not about reed instruments (eg horns, flutes); and to separate works on flutes from general works on woodwinds by all the works about particular brass instruments; all these show that the compilers of this section of DC18 did not understand their job.

To finish off our attack on this example, we might point out that although the class SINGLE-REED INSTRUMENTS (eg clarinets, saxophones) has been enumerated, the class DOUBLE-REED INSTRUMENTS (eg oboes, bassoons) is not available, and the classifier is instructed to class works on this subject in 788.056! Perhaps there is something in the conspiracy theory, after all.

Apart from these inefficiencies, which are more likely to occur in enumerative schemes, faceted schemes have two more advantages. The first is that it is much easier to insert newly-discovered classes into a faceted classification scheme; if the new class is a compound of elemental classes already present in the scheme, no more work needs to be done; if it involves new elemental classes only these need to be added— eg, if we discovered the new concept Tortoises, we need only add the class TORTOISES to our 'animals by zoologists' taxonomy' subfacet, following the class REPTILES. In an enumerative scheme new compound and superimposed classes must be given their special places, whether or not their elemental classes are already present; and if we add a new elemental class we must also be prepared to add all the new superimposed and compound classes which it will generate. So, if we add TORTOISES, at some stage we must add LAND TORTOISES, PHYSIOLOGY OF TORTOISES, REPRODUCTION OF WATER TORTOISES and so on.

The second advantage is that it is much easier for the compiler of a faceted scheme to allow the classifier to choose how documents in his library are to be grouped, than it is for the compiler of an enumerative scheme—the enumerative scheme tends to be more inflexible. Both of these points will be discussed in more detail later.

We should note two points in favour of the enumerative scheme before we leave it; the first is that synthesis often produces longer and more complicated notations than those given to enumerated classes; the second, that a faceted scheme requires the classifier to think more—but this should not, perhaps, be regarded as a disadvantage.

For the reasons discussed in this chapter, most modern special classification schemes are compiled using faceted principles—those which we are to discuss in this book. In addition, there are two faceted general schemes. Dr Ranganathan's *Colon classification* is the test-bed on which he tried out his principles of classification, on which so much of the modern theory of library classification is based; and the second edition of Bliss's *Bibliographic classification* began to appear in 1977, from the work of the (British) Bliss Classification Association led by Mr J Mills—this is perhaps the first general faceted scheme which could be regarded as a challenger to the stranglehold of DC.

Lastly we must remember that so-called enumerative schemes may contain provision for a great deal of synthesis. By the second edition of DC, Melvil Dewey had realised that the enumeration of forms of presentation under subjects is wasteful—this may seem obvious, but it still occurs in LC:

Eugenics
    Periodicals
    Congresses
    Exhibitions

    Scientific (works)
        General works
        Heredity

    Popular (works)
        General
        Special

Limitation of offspring
Periodicals
Biography
General works

(Note that in this sequence only two of the enumerated classes represent subject subdivisions of EUGENICS.) By DC2, then, Dewey had begun to provide a table of common subdivisions for concepts of form such as periodicals, whose notation could be added to that of any subject class. In DC18, faceted principles have been heavily—although inconsistently and often clumsily—used; as in this selection from the class Zoology:

591.1   Physiology
591.12   Respiration
591.16   Reproduction

592   Invertebrates
595.7   Insects *

596   Vertebrates
598.1   Reptiles *
598.13   Tortoises *

which includes the instruction that those classes marked * should synthesise notation from the section 591.1-591.8, by adding to the number for the animal the digits 04 followed by the digits which come after 591 as appropriate; for example, THE RESPIRATION OF TORTOISES would be expressed by 598.130412. Even with this facility, it is still not possible to specify classes such as INVERTEBRATE REPRODUCTION or RESPIRATION OF VERTEBRATES, as it would be with a true faceted scheme.

REFERENCES
1 These terms are found throughout Ranganathan's works.

FOUR

DECISIONS

SUPPOSE, then, that we need to construct a classification scheme in a limited area of knowledge, and that we have decided that it should be in faceted form. What decisions would we have to make? Ironically, it is the model of the enumerative scheme in the previous chapter which better illustrates these, because the results of making them are explicitly shown in the scheme itself—the results of the same decisions taken in the construction of the faceted scheme would not all appear until the scheme had been used to classify a collection of documents. The choices made in order to produce the enumerative scheme were these: if a document could be placed in two or more classes, because it deals with more than one elemental class, which should we prefer—we may call this 'choice of citation order'; second, what filing order should we choose between classes which are coordinate with each other—we may call this 'choice of order in array'; third, what filing order should we choose between classes in a broader-narrower relationship; fourth, what filing order should we choose between collateral classes.

Citation order
The purpose of a classification scheme is to show relationships by collocation—that is, to keep related classes more or less together according to the closeness of the relationship; for example, the classes WATER INVERTEBRATES and LAND INVERTEBRATES are close together in our model scheme, and documents dealing with these classes would be placed physically close to each other on shelves, because they both are about invertebrates. Paradoxically, though, any classification scheme must scatter documents on many more

classes than those whose documents it collocates; for example, if we decide to keep together all works on invertebrates, we have to accept that all documents on land animals will not be collocated—those which deal with land invertebrates will be found in the class INVERTEBRATES, as happens in our scheme. Again, the same decision results in the scattering of works on, say, respiration—only works on respiration in general will be found in the class RESPIRATION, because we have decided that works on respiration of invertebrates shall be placed in the class INVERTEBRATES. If we look at the scheme we can see that while all classes dealing with insects are in one group, the class PHYSIOLOGY is scattered in fifteen different places, and the class LAND ANIMALS in five—LAND ANIMALS itself, which takes documents on the subject in general, and LAND INVERTEBRATES, LAND INSECTS, LAND VERTEBRATES and LAND REPTILES. These scattered subjects are called 'distributed relatives'(1).

The choice of citation order, then, determines which classes are to have their documents kept together, and which are to have theirs scattered—and to what extent. The term is derived from faceted classification, and refers to the order in which elemental classes are cited when assembling them to form a superimposed or composite class—the class cited first being that whose documents are collocated, and that cited last being the class whose documents are most scattered. In an enumerative scheme it means the order in which 'characteristics of division' are applied to the universe which is to be divided up; this produces the same result, as the following simplified hierarchy shows:

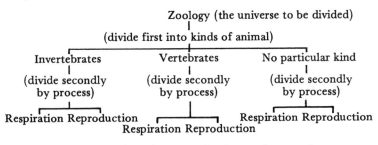

This demonstrates that, by our citation order, works on, say, INVERTEBRATES will be found together; but that works on RESPIRATION will be found in three different places.

38

The obvious basis for choice of citation order is, of course, the needs of our clients. If our scheme is to be used in a zoological research library whose clients are primarily interested in animal processes rather than the animals themselves, then our suggested citation order would be unhelpful, and we should instead cite a process before an animal; but in a general library, the citation order we have used is probably the more helpful. Where it is not possible to determine the needs of our clients, we can use general principles developed by Bliss, Ranganathan, Coates and others(2). These include the principle of decreasing concreteness (that the more concrete should be cited before the less concrete—eg Animals before Processes); the principle of purpose or end-product (that a class which represents the purpose of the study of the subject should be cited before any other—eg, if knowledge about animals is the result of studying Zoology, then a class of animal should be cited before, say, a class of process or a class of operation); the principle of consensus (that the citation order should conform to the way in which the structure of the subject is thought about by educated people, and especially to the way in which it is taught); and the wall-picture principle (that a dependent topic should be cited after the class on which it depends—eg, in the class EXPERIMENTS ON REPTILES the animal should be cited before the operation, because you cannot carry out an operation until you have something to operate on, just as you cannot paint a picture on a wall until you have a wall to paint it on). It may be that different principles would suggest different citation orders; for example, in Agriculture the principle of purpose would give the order Crop-Operation, but it seems likely that in agricultural colleges students study agricultural operations, giving the citation order, according to the principle of consensus, Operation-Crop. Despite this, a general citation order has been suggested(3), following from principles such as we have given above; this is Thing-Part-Constituent-Property-Material-Action-Agent of action. For his CC, Ranganathan imposes for most main classes the citation order Personality-Matter-Energy-Space-Time (usually abbreviated to PMEST), and assigns each of the facets in the class to one or other of these five fundamental categories.

39

Order in array

An array is a set of coordinate classes; for example, the classes INVERTEBRATES and VERTEBRATES form an array, as do WATER REPTILES and LAND REPTILES. A classification scheme is an ordered set of classes; and we must, therefore, could place an array in random order, or in alphabetical order (as LC often does), but neither of these is helpful—neither, of itself, displays relationships. Principles for the choice of helpful order in array vary according to the subject; they include chronological order and the very similar developmental order, in which classes which occur later in time file after earlier classes (eg, from a zoology classification, the array KILLING, PRESERVATION OF DEAD SPECIMENS, DISPLAY OF DEAD SPECIMENS; from an architecture scheme an array of styles ROMANESQUE, GOTHIC, RENAISSANCE; and from a scheme for librarianship, ACQUISITION, INDEXING, CIRCULATION, WITHDRAWAL); spatial order (eg, from a classification for astronomy, an excerpt from the array of planets in order from the Sun: MERCURY, VENUS, EARTH, MARS . . . ; from a scheme for zoology, POLAR ANIMALS, TEMPERATE ZONE ANIMALS, TROPICAL ANIMALS); an order of increasing complexity (eg SOLITARY ANIMALS, HERD ANIMALS, SOCIAL ANIMALS—an order which moves from animals who have very little social interaction to animals which live in very highly organised communities with, for example, specialisation of function—a move from the simple to the complex); an order of increasing size; and, as a last example, what Ranganathan calls 'canonical order'(4), that is an order sanctioned by its use by subject experts.

A striking example of canonical order is provided by a Loughborough student, James Langridge, who undertook an evaluation of the draft schedule for Astronomy of BC2 for his third-year major project 1977-78. Among the changes he recommended was the reversal of the order in array for the subfacet 'Stars by spectral type', to agree with the order of a mnemonic by which astronomers remember these types of star; this mnemonic—'O be a fine girl kiss me right now smack'—would only be known to astronomers, and the order

40

in an array which results from following it is, therefore, a canonical order; one which only astronomers would appreciate.

As we have suggested, different subjects may yield different bases for order in array. The decisions we had to make in order to produce our model enumerative scheme, and the bases on which we made them, were these: the order between RESPIRATION and REPRODUCTION (we filed the more immediate need before the less immediate—if you do not breathe you die very quickly, if you stop reproducing you may still have a long, although perhaps unsatisfactory, life as an individual specimen); the order between WATER ANIMALS and LAND ANIMALS (life probably began in water and organisms later moved on to land, so our order in array follows this progression); and the order between INVERTEBRATES and VERTEBRATES (a developmental order—vertebrates developed later than invertebrates, and our order in array reflects this). The same principles were followed when placing coordinate superimposed or compound classes in order; eg RESPIRATION OF WATER ANIMALS files before REPRODUCTION OF WATER ANIMALS, and WATER REPTILES files before LAND REPTILES.

Broader-narrower order
It is a well-known principle, followed intuitively even by those who have had no education in information work, that broader classes should file before narrower; if a layman stood before a shelf of books on Sport, and found himself looking at works on ball games, he would, without thinking, move towards the right to find works on, say, cricket or soccer, and to the left if he wanted works on sport in general. Our model enumerative scheme displays this helpful order; for example, INVERTEBRATES files before INSECTS, because the latter is a species of the former, and is wholly contained by it; similarly, PHYSIOLOGY OF INSECTS is narrower than INSECTS (although the one is not a species of the other), and RESPIRATION OF INSECTS is narrower than PHYSIOLOGY OF INSECTS; and the relationship of subordination between the three classes is displayed by their order. The problem of the filing order between INSECTS and PHYSIOLOGY OF INVERTEBRATES, neither of which is broader than the other (although both are subordinate to INVERTEBRATES), and which are not coordinate classes

41

so that we cannot choose an order in array, is dealt with in the next section.

It is worth mentioning that some schemes allow the classifier to choose to file classes in narrower-broader order; there seems little point in this, except that, for a reason discussed in the next section, it will bring works on classes cited first in the citation order—which might be considered to be the most important—to the beginning of the sequence rather than the end.

Order between collateral classes
Collateral classes are either different kinds of things with the same parent class (eg the classes PHYSIOLOGY and WATER ANIMALS); kinds of the same thing produced by the application of different characteristics of division (eg the classes WATER ANIMALS—a kind of animal defined by habitat—and HIBERNATING ANIMALS—a kind of animal defined by habit); or kinds of the same thing produced by one characteristic, but not sharing the same immediate superordinate class (eg the classes INSECTS and REPTILES). These classes are not in a relationship of inclusion—one is not superordinate to another—nor do they form an array. In the third case, however, the immediate superordinate classes of INSECTS and REPTILES (that is INVERTE-BRATES and VERTEBRATES) do form an array for which we have already chosen a filing order, and the two subordinate classes naturally fall into place in this. In the first two cases, though, this cannot happen, and we have to find some other principle on which to base the filing order between collateral classes of these types.

If we take the filing order between the two classes LAND ANIMALS and INVERTEBRATES as our example, we can begin by noting that in our enumerative scheme there are many more subordinate classes grouped with INVERTE-BRATES than there are grouped with LAND ANIMALS—eleven for the first, three for the second. We can also see that some of the classes subordinate to INVERTEBRATES are narrower than some of the classes grouped with LAND ANIMALS—for example, PHYSIOLOGY OF LAND IN-VERTEBRATES is narrower than PHYSIOLOGY OF LAND

42

ANIMALS, and narrower than LAND ANIMALS itself, of course. The reverse, though, is not true: no class grouped with LAND ANIMALS is narrower than any class grouped with INVERTEBRATES. This situation results from our choice of citation order; when we have a work which could be collocated either with other works on land animals or with other works on invertebrates, because it deals with land invertebrates, we have made the decision to place it with the class INVERTEBRATES—so that some works on land animals are not found in the class LAND ANIMALS, but in the class INVERTEBRATES.

Now, if it is true, as we stated above, that broader-narrower order is helpful, we ought to file a group of classes, some of which are narrower than classes in another group after that group; otherwise we shall have narrower classes filing before broader. For example, if the invertebrate group were to file before the land animals group, then the class PHYSIOLOGY OF LAND INVERTEBRATES would file before the broader classes PHYSIOLOGY OF LAND ANIMALS and LAND ANIMALS. We must, then, file the land animals group of classes before the invertebrates group; consequently, we must file the class LAND ANIMALS before its collateral class IN-VERTEBRATES; and this is the principle by which the filing order of collateral classes of the first two types is decided.

We might note that if our citation order is INVERTE-BRATES—LAND ANIMALS, then the filing order between the collateral classes is LAND ANIMALS—INVERTE-BRATES; so that we may call our principle the 'principle of inversion', and state it in these terms: if broader-narrower order between classes and documents is required, then the filing order between collateral classes of the first two types must be the reverse of their citation order.(5)

As we hinted earlier in this chapter, it is possible to make collateral classes file in the same order as their citation order. If we do this we shall produce narrower-broader order, of course; this brings documents on classes cited first to the beginning of the sequence rather than to the end. There seems to be no practical advantage to this, and it is contrary to our clients' expectations; but, as we said earlier, some schemes do allow classifiers to make the choice.

43

REFERENCES

1 Savage, Ernest *Manual of book classification and display* Allen & Unwin, 1946.

2 see the textbooks Mills, J *Modern outline of library classification* Chapman & Hall, 1960; and Foskett, A C *Subject approach to information* 3rd ed, Bingley, 1977.

3 Foskett, A C *The Universal Decimal Classification* Bingley, 1973.

4 Ranganathan, S R *Prolegomena to library classification* 3rd ed, Bombay; London, Asia Publishing House, 1967.

5 see the standard textbooks on the principle of inversion —especially Mills; also Langridge, Derek *Approach to classification for students of librarianship* Bingley, 1973.

FIVE

THE CONSTRUCTION OF A FACETED SCHEME: I

AS WE have seen, the construction of a faceted scheme is very much easier than that of an enumerative scheme, although the decisions discussed in the last chapter must be made for faceted schemes too. A faceted scheme lists elemental classes only; in these schemes such classes are called 'foci' (singular: focus)(1). Foci are organised to form 'facets'; a facet consists of all the foci which are kinds of the same thing, and that thing gives the facet its name. For example, a classification scheme for architecture will have a facet containing foci such as CHURCHES, TIMBER BUILDINGS, CASTLES, GOTHIC BUILDINGS, and this is called the Buildings facet; it will have another listing foci such as FOUNDATIONS, WINDOWS, BUTTRESSES, VAULTS, and this is called the Parts facet. In a classification scheme for social welfare there will be a Persons facet, containing foci such as CHILDREN, IMMIGRANTS, MIDDLE CLASS PEOPLE, FEMALES; a Problems facet, with foci such as HOMELESSNESS, MENTAL ILLNESS, LONELINESS, POVERTY, CRIME; and a Therapies facet, containing such foci as PLAY THERAPY, GUARANTEED MINIMUM INCOME, PRISON, ADOPTION. The term 'facet' is used in its common meaning of 'aspect'—people are one aspect of the subject of social welfare, their problems another and the treatment of these problems a third. The term 'focus' seems to be a metaphor from optics(2); we could say that in the subject statement Play Therapy for Maladjustment, the Therapies facet and the Problems facet are 'in focus'—that is, that the document deals precisely with these aspects; but the Persons facet is not 'in focus'—the image of this facet is blurred, because the document does not deal specifically with any particular kind of person.

45

We can see from the examples above that it may be possible to have groupings of foci within a facet; for example, in the Buildings facet of architecture we could see the basis of three groups—a group consisting of buildings defined by purpose, with foci such as CHURCHES, CASTLES, HOUSES, SCHOOLS; a group consisting of buildings defined by their material (TIMBER BUILDINGS, STONE BUILDINGS, GLASS BUILDINGS . . .); and a group defined by style (ROMANESQUE BUILDINGS, GOTHIC BUILDINGS, RENAISSANCE BUILDINGS . . .). Similarly, in the Persons facet of social welfare we can see the possibility of grouping by age, by place of origin, by class, by sex, by occupation, by religion and so on. These groups are called 'subfacets'; a subfacet is defined as the set of foci produced by the application of one characteristic of division—eg buildings 'by use', persons 'by age'. It is intriguing (but not particularly important) to note that any subfacet can contain all the things which the whole facet contains; this sounds like putting a quart into a pint pot, but subfacets are merely different views of the same set of things—for example, any building is composed of building materials, and, therefore, all buildings can be accommodated in the Buildings by material subfacet; any building has a use, so all buildings can be accommodated in the Buildings by use subfacet; any person must be either male or female, so the Persons by sex subfacet can contain all persons; and so on.

Now that we have established the terms 'foci', 'facet' and 'subfacet', we can outline the stages in the construction of a faceted scheme for a special area of knowledge, and then illustrate these by producing a scheme. The stages are these:

1 examine a representative sample of literature, to discover the elemental classes its authors deal with;

2 group these 'isolates'(3) (that is, as-yet-unorganised elemental classes) into facets, when they become foci;

3 if necessary, apply different characteristics of division to facets to produce subfacets;

4 place the foci in each facet or in each subfacet into order, using broader-narrower order for foci in that relationship or an appropriate order in array for coordinate foci;

5 place the subfacets in order in their facets (their foci are collateral classes of the second type, so that we can use the principle of inversion in deciding this order);

6 choose a filing order between facets (their foci are collateral classes of the first type, so again we can use the principle of inversion).

At this stage we shall have done enough to produce a scheme which will result in a preferred collocation and systematic order of documents or of records of documents; however, to make its use easier we must do two more things:

7 add a code to each class which will act as its address, showing its filing position; this code is called 'notation'; and

8 produce an alphabetical index to the order of classes, using their notation as a link.

As we suggested earlier, we shall demonstrate these steps by constructing a classification scheme for Zoology. It will not be a complete scheme, of course, because that would take up too much space; we shall assume that the following set of documents contains all the classes which we must accommodate—together with some common-sense extensions to the list, which we shall mention:

1   A closer look at butterflies and moths
2   Essays on the physiology of marine fauna
3   Animals of the mountains
4   Laboratory experiments in the respiration of
        vertebrates
5   Social behaviour in animals
6   The amphibian visual system
7   Things that sting (about venomous animals)
8   Littoral fauna
9   How mammals run
10   Raptors
11   Amphibious animals
12   The role of play in the development of primates
13   Birds of the coast
14   The insect integument
15   Animals of the sea shore
16   The senses of sea mammals

17 Birds of prey
18 Desert reptiles
19 Sensory adaptations of the skin in colobus monkeys
20 Migratory birds
21 The generic names of moths of the world
22 The flight of the honeybee
23 The nutritional requirements of the panda
24 Salt water fish
25 The butterfly brain
26 Invertebrates of rivers and streams
27 Nature's wonders of the lowlands
28 Tropical leaf moths
29 Birds of the woodlands
30 The life of a golden eagle
31 Entomological taxonomy (a periodical on the classification of insects)
32 Hibernation
33 Agression in man
34 The intelligence of rats
35 Equatorial snakes
36 The panda
37 How to collect and identify spiders
38 Migration in birds
39 A comparison between frogs and toads
40 Mammalian reproduction

We can take each of these titles (except two) as accurate subject statements, and analyse each into its component elemental classes. While doing this we must remember

(1) to recognise synonyms (eg animals/fauna; raptors/birds of prey; littoral fauna/animals of the sea shore), so as not to create more than one class for the same concept;

(2) to differentiate between homonyms or near-homonyms, to ensure that different concepts form different classes (eg, we must not confuse 'pandas' in document (23) with 'pandas' in document (36)—the works are about two quite different animals which happen to have the same name; similarly, 'amphibious animals' are not the same as 'amphibians'; and, if we were creating a scheme for use in a general library, it would be unhelpful and disrespectful to keep a work about

48

the Archbishop of Canterbury close to document (12), because they are both about primates); and

(3) to distinguish between superimposed classes and compound classes (eg between MIGRATORY BIRDS and MIGRATION IN BIRDS), so that we can arrange for both kinds of class to be expressible by our scheme.

As we shall recognise elemental classes by their representing a kind of thing, we might as well assign them to facets as we recognise them—a facet, remember, being a set of classes all of which are kinds of the same thing. Thus, document (1) is polytopical; it deals with two distinct elemental classes. Each of these is a kind of animal, so this document has yielded two foci for our Animals facet. Document (2) not only gives us another focus for the same facet—the class MARINE ANIMALS—but also suggests two more facets: Physiology is a kind of process, so that we should have a Processes facet, and Essays is the form in which this document presents its information, so that we should have a Form of presentation facet which will enable us, if we wish, to subdivide a set of documents on the same subject according to their form (document (31) also gives us a focus for the Form facet).

Documents (3) and (4) give us yet more foci for the Animals facet—MOUNTAIN ANIMALS and VERTEBRATES —while (4) adds both another focus for the Processes facet and a focus for a new facet which we might call Operations. For a change, the Animals facet is not in focus in (5)—this work does not deal with any particular animal; however, Social Behaviour is a kind of activity, so we now have an Activities facet. When we come to superimposed classes, we must remember to analyse these into their elemental classes too, even though they will be in the same facet; for example, (18) gives us two foci for the Animals facet—the classes DESERT ANIMALS and REPTILES, and (24) gives us SEA/MARINE/SALT WATER ANIMALS as well as FISH.

The result of the analysis of the subjects of the documents is the following list of classes, arranged in facets:

(Animals facet)
  Butterflies
  Moths
  Marine/Sea/Salt water animals
  Mountain animals
  Vertebrates
  Animals/Fauna
  Amphibians
  Venomous animals
  Littoral fauna/Animals of the sea shore
  Mammals
  Raptors/Birds of prey
  Amphibious animals
  Primates
  Birds
  Coastal animals
  Insects
  Desert Animals
  Reptiles
  Colobus monkeys
  Migratory animals
  Honeybees
  Pandas (a kind of bear)
  Fish
  Invertebrates
  River animals
  Lowland animals
  Tropical animals
  Leaf moths
  Woodland animals
  Golden eagles
  Man
  Rats
  Equatorial animals
  Snakes
  Pandas (an animal related to kinkajous and raccoons, and not to bears)
  Spiders
  Frogs
  Toads

(Physiological processes and parts facet—combined, because it seems unhelpful to separate, for example, the part 'eyes' from the process 'sight')
  Physiology
  Respiration
  Visual system (this demonstrates the necessity of the combined facet—a system includes both parts and processes; perhaps, though, a work about a 'visual system' is just a work about Sight, and we should include that term here as a synonym)
  Running
  Integument/Skin (are these really synonyms? The integument of a colobus monkey is certainly skin, but that of an insect is its exoskeleton; still, as they are probably both studied as outer coverings we will treat them as synonymous)
  Senses (ie sensory system)
  Flight (ie flying, not fleeing)
  Nutrition/Feeding
  Brain
  Reproduction

(Activities/Behaviour facet)
  Activities/Behaviour
  Social behaviour
  Play
  Hibernation
  Migration
(is the distinction we have made between things which animals do—the foci in the Activities facet—and what happens *in* the animal—the foci in the Processes facet—valid? Let us assume so).

(Form of presentation facet)
  Essays
  Periodicals

(Operations facet—things done to animals)
  Laboratory experiments
  Naming/nomenclature
  Classification
  Collection
  Identification (is this the same as Naming? No, surely Naming would follow Identification)

(Attributes of animals facet)
    Aggression
    Intelligence

(General processes facet)
    Development/Maturation
    Adaptation

You will have noticed that some 'thinking aloud' and some justifications have been included in this draft, as we would when drafting a real scheme. The decision to have a separate Activities facet was made intuitively; its formal justification is that it is possible to have a compound class involving foci from the Processes facet and from the Activities facet—eg, RESPIRATION DURING HIBERNATION or SOCIAL BEHAVIOUR IN FEEDING; when this is so we must have separate facets—it proves that more than one kind of thing is involved (also, if we do not have two facets, our filing order will not be based on the principle of inversion). On the other hand, it is not possible to have compound classes whose elements are foci from the Processes and parts facet, so these can form a combined facet.

The next stage is to consider whether any of the facets can be divided by more than one characteristic of division; if it is possible to do so that facet must be divided into sub-facets. In fact, it looks as though only the Animals facet needs subfacets—for example, MIGRATORY ANIMALS is clearly a class defined by behaviour, while WOODLAND ANIMALS is a class defined by habitat. We can add the same justification that we used for having separate Processes and Activities facets—that it is possible to imagine a class containing both elemental classes, in this case the superimposed class MIGRATORY WOODLAND ANIMALS; and we must, therefore, place them in separate groups.

The characteristics of division operating in the Animals facet seem to be these: habitat (shown in the class MOUNTAIN ANIMALS); effect on man (shown in the class VENOMOUS ANIMALS); behaviour or habit (MIGRATORY ANIMALS); and a fourth, which is difficult to name, but whose application produces the familiar species of animal, such as the classes BUTTERFLIES, VERTEBRATES, MAMMALS, REPTILES and INSECTS. We have, in fact, already

52

used a name for this characteristic, which we have not yet explained. Species of animal of the kind listed are defined by zoologists using complex criteria; for example, while it is easy to define MOUNTAIN ANIMALS as 'animals which live in mountains', the definition of, say, the class INSECTS requires more: insects are invertebrate animals with a body divided into three distinct sections and having six legs. We could, therefore, name the characteristic for this subfacet 'zoologists' taxonomy'—that is, its foci are those produced by the classificatory activities of zoologists. The term is accurate, although clumsy, and we have adopted it.

At this stage in the construction of our scheme we must be mindful of Aristotle's rules of logical division which, if followed, ensure the efficient derivation of the species of a genus, which is the process we are now engaged in(4). The rule which is applicable to our present operation is that only one characteristic of division should be applied at a time. Translated into our situation, this means that all the foci in one subfacet must be produced by the application of only one characteristic. There is, of course, no reason why we should do otherwise; but some schemes do ignore this rule, and their efficiency suffers as a result. The two bad results are cross-classification (that is, the provision of more than one possibly valid class for a concept) and its reverse—failure to provide a class for a concept. Consider this sequence from LEC2—the foci are from the Educands facet (that is, people who are being educated):

Svj Teenagers

(educands beyond usual age of formal education)
Swb Adult
Swd Parent
Swf Housewife
Swg Older person

It is quite clear that more than one characteristic has been applied to produce this set of foci; three of the foci listed are classes representing people by age, one focus represents people by relationship, and one, people by occupation. As a result the classes are not mutually exclusive—a housewife may well be an older person and a parent as well—and there is no indication of which is the preferred place for a superimposed

53

class such as OLDER PERSON WHO IS ALSO A HOUSE-WIFE WHO IS ALSO A PARENT. What is more, because of this confusion, it is not possible to express the class TEEN-AGERS WHO ARE PARENTS—the only class representing the concept Parents is enumerated in a sequence based on age, headed 'educands beyond usual age of formal education'. Adherence to the rule of logical division mentioned will produce subfacets whose foci are mutually exclusive classes, and avoid these problems. Further, it will ensure that the filing order between classes has been thought about in relation to citation order—that is, that the principle of inversion will be observed; this is not possible when foci produced by different characteristics are jumbled up in one sequence, as in the LEC2 example. Let us, then, apply each of the four characteristics we discovered to the Animals facet; this is the result:

(Animals facet)
　　Animals/Fauna

　　　　　　　　　(Animals by habitat subfacet)
　　　　　　　　　　Marine/Sea/Salt water animals
　　　　　　　　　　Mountain animals
　　　　　　　　　　Littoral Fauna/Animals of the sea shore
　　　　　　　　　　Amphibious animals
(Animals by effect　Coastal animals
　on man subfacet)　Desert animals
　Venomous animals　River animals　　　　(Animals by habit
　　　　　　　　　　Lowland animals　　　　subfacet)
　　　　　　　　　　Tropical animals　　　　　Migratory animals
　　　　　　　　　　Woodland animals
　　　　　　　　　　Equatorial animals

　　　　　　(Animals by zoologists' taxonomy subfacet)
　　　Butterflies　　　　　　　Pandas (a kind of bear)
　　　Moths　　　　　　　　　Fish
　　　Vertebrates　　　　　　　Invertebrates
　　　Amphibians　　　　　　　Leaf moths
　　　Mammals　　　　　　　　Golden eagles
　　　Raptors/Birds of prey　　　Man
　　　Primates　　　　　　　　Rats
　　　Birds　　　　　　　　　Snakes
　　　Insects　　　　　　　　Pandas (not a kind of bear)
　　　Reptiles　　　　　　　　Spiders
　　　Colobus monkeys　　　　　Frogs
　　　Honeybees　　　　　　　Toads

Now we must apply another rule of logical division. This is that division by a characteristic must be exhaustive—we must include all the classes produced by each characteristic, or our scheme will be incomplete. As we have already agreed that our scheme should not be a complete one, to save space, let us give token obedience to this rule, and add only a few classes to each subfacet. The focus in the 'animals by effect on man' subfacet is clearly harmful, so we might add the class BENEFICIAL ANIMALS. To 'animals by habit' we shall add HIBERNATING ANIMALS (especially as we have the class HIBERNATION in the Activities facet); to 'animals by habitat' UPLAND ANIMALS, HILL ANIMALS, JUNGLE ANIMALS, LAKE ANIMALS, GRASSLAND ANIMALS, POLAR ANIMALS, TEMPERATE ZONE ANIMALS and SCRUBLAND ANIMALS. To 'animals by zoologists' taxonomy' let us add at this stage only some companions for the class SNAKES — LIZARDS and TORTOISES.

The third rule of logical division is also about not omitting classes. This states that division must be proximate; that is, that no superordinate class should be left out. If this rule is not observed we say that the chain of broader-narrower classes does not modulate; or that there is a leap in division. Failure to modulate results not only in inability to express the omitted classes, but also in the possibility of the compiler of the scheme not recognising relationships. Look at this hierarchy, which represents some of the relationships in our 'animals by zoologists' taxonomy' subfacet:

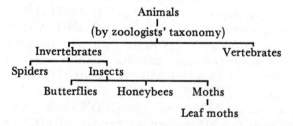

Here, the chain Animals—Invertebrates—Insects—Butterflies does not modulate — classes which are narrower than IN-SECTS but broader than classes on the next step have been omitted. For example, between INSECTS and BUTTER-FLIES, LEPIDOPTERA has been left out; and between

55

INSECTS and HONEYBEES two steps are missing—HYMEN-OPTERA, a class which includes ants and bees, and BEES. Naturally, these forgotten classes cannot be expressed; but their omission has also led the compiler of the scheme to obscure the close relationship between BUTTERFLIES and MOTHS (both of which are kinds of Lepidoptera) by placing HONEYBEES (which is not a kind of Lepidoptera) between them. A better hierarchy, one which modulates, would look like this:

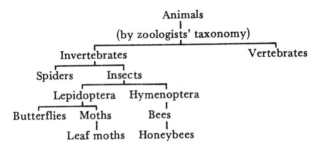

Let us look for omissions of this kind, and insert classes where necessary—although, once again, we shall only do this selectively. In the 'animals by effect on man' subfacet we have certainly left out the class HARMFUL ANIMALS, which is obviously superordinate to VENOMOUS ANIMALS; similarly, in the 'habitat' subfacet we have failed to include the class WATER/AQUATIC ANIMALS, superordinate to MARINE ANIMALS, and although we have LAKE ANIMALS and RIVER ANIMALS we have not included FRESH WATER ANIMALS. (Having included AQUATIC ANIMALS, by the way, it seems reasonable to put in LAND ANIMALS). Lastly, in the 'zoologists' taxonomy' subfacet (in which we have already corrected some omissions of this kind) we still find that we need to add EAGLES, ARACHNIDS (a class which includes SPIDERS), BEARS (because we have its subordinate class PANDAS), PROCYONIDAE (the class which includes the other kind of panda), MONKEYS and RODENTS (of course, in a real scheme we would find many more, but these will do for demonstration purposes).

We have now organised the foci in the Animals facet into subfacets, obeying the rules of logical division to ensure that we have done so efficiently. Unfortunately, this does not complete the process of grouping in this facet, because the 'animals by habitat' subfacet should itself be divided into four subfacets—each of which will contain foci representing habitats produced by one characteristic of division. These characteristics are 'by latitude' (giving foci such as POLAR ANIMALS, TROPICAL ANIMALS); 'by element' (WATER ANIMALS, LAND ANIMALS); 'by landform' (MOUNTAIN ANIMALS, LOWLAND ANIMALS); and 'by ground cover' (DESERT ANIMALS, JUNGLE ANIMALS). Again, the need for these subfacets is shown by the possibility of super-imposed classes taking elements from each; it is quite probable that there is a work on the class WATER ANIMALS OF TROPICAL JUNGLES, or LAND ANIMALS OF EQUA-TORIAL MOUNTAINS.

The result of our grouping of the foci in the Animals facet into subfacets can be seen on page 58.

As we said earlier, none of the other facets require this treatment because they do not display more than one characteristic of division. It follows that the first rule of logical division does not apply to them; but the other two, concerning the omission of classes, do. So, as a token gesture, let us add just two more foci to the Operations facet—the class EXPERIMENTS, which is superordinate to the class LAB-ORATORY EXPERIMENTS; and two more foci to the Processes facet: the class LOCOMOTION, which is super-ordinate to both RUNNING and FLYING; and NERVOUS SYSTEM. Apart from that, we shall leave the other facets as they appear earlier, and move on to the next stage in the construction of our scheme.

REFERENCES

1 Ranganathan, S R *Elements of library classification* 2nd ed, AAL, 1959.

2 Ibid (see pages 57-58).

3 Ibid.

4 Mills. op cit.

(Animals facet)
Animals/Fauna

(Animals by effect on man subfacet)
Harmful animals
Beneficial animals
Venomous animals

(by latitude)
Equatorial animals
Temperate animals
Polar animals
Tropical animals

(Animals by habitat subfacet)

(by element)
Aquatic/Water animals
River animals
Land animals
Marine animals
Lake animals
Amphibious animals
Fresh water animals

(by land form)
Mountain animals
Lowland animals
Littoral fauna
Coastal animals
Hill animals

(Animals by habit subfacet)
Migratory animals
Hibernating animals

(by ground cover)
Jungle animals
Desert animals
Woodland animals
Grassland animals
Scrubland animals

(Animals by zoologists' taxonomy subfacet)

Butterflies	Rats
Moths	Snakes
Vertebrates	Pandas (not bears)
Amphibians	Spiders
Mammals	Frogs
Raptors	Toads
Primates	Lizards
Birds	Tortoises
Insects	Lepidoptera
Reptiles	Hymenoptera
Colobus monkeys	Bees
Honeybees	Eagles
Pandas (bears)	Arachnids
Fish	Bears
Invertebrates	Procyonidae
Leaf moths	Monkeys
Golden eagles	Rodents
Man	

SIX

THE CONSTRUCTION OF A FACETED SCHEME: II

HAVING grouped our foci, we must now put them in order within the groups. As we have done so much with the 'animals by habitat' subfacet, we could use its own subfacets and their foci to illustrate the principles involved. Take the 'by latitude' subfacet first. In it, we can see a genus-species relationship: equatorial animals are obviously a kind of tropical animal, and we should collocate the two classes, placing them in broader-narrower order:

Tropical animals
  Equatorial animals

However, there is no broader-narrower relationship between the classes TEMPERATE ZONE ANIMALS, POLAR ANIMALS and TROPICAL ANIMALS; these are coordinate classes, and we shall have to choose an order in array for them. An appropriate basis for order between concepts involving geography is spatial proximity, and we would apply it intuitively, choosing either a movement from the equator to the poles:

Tropical animals
  Equatorial animals
Temperate zone animals
Polar animals

or the reverse:

Polar animals
Temperate zone animals
Tropical animals
  Equatorial animals

Let us choose the second, as it seems more natural to move from colder to warmer; and besides, the first seems to

59

interrupt the progression, by going from tropics to equator before going on to temperate zones.

In the 'by element' subfacet the same principles apply, although it is a little more complicated. We shall want to display the genus-species relationships:

> Aquatic animals   Land animals   Amphibious animals
>   River animals
>   Marine animals
>   Lake animals
>   Fresh water animals

but there is a further relationship of this kind:

>   Aquatic animals
> Marine animals   Fresh water animals
>   Lake animals   River animals

We can now choose orders in array. The first is that between LAKE ANIMALS and RIVER ANIMALS. As rivers tend to flow into lakes, we will have the order

> River animals
> Lake animals

Next, we have to place the classes MARINE ANIMALS and FRESH WATER ANIMALS (with its subordinate classes RIVER ANIMALS, LAKE ANIMALS) in order. As seas are usually much larger bodies of water than fresh water, let us place them in an order of increasing size, giving us:

> Aquatic animals
>   Fresh water animals
>   River animals
>   Lake animals
>   Marine animals

Lastly, we have to choose the order between the coordinate classes AQUATIC ANIMALS, LAND ANIMALS and AM-PHIBIOUS ANIMALS. As life probably began in water, let us file water animals before land animals; and as amphibious animals are both land and water animals, we will file this class between the other two. Our final order of classes in this subfacet, then, is:

Aquatic animals
   Fresh water animals
      River animals
      Lake animals
   Marine animals
Amphibious animals
Land animals

We suggest the following orders for the remaining subfacets in the 'animals by habitat' subfacet: perhaps you can see the basis for the orders in array:

(by land form)	(by ground cover)
Coastal animals	Desert animals
Littoral animals	Grassland animals
Lowland animals	Scrubland animals
Upland animals	Woodland animals
Hill animals	Jungle animals
Mountain animals	

Before we do the same thing for the other subfacets and facets, let us complete our work on the 'animals by habitat' subfacet. We cannot claim that we have placed the classes in order until we have placed the subfacets in order—otherwise, how can we say that LOWLAND ANIMALS files before or after GRASSLAND ANIMALS, or FRESHWATER ANIMALS before or after TROPICAL ANIMALS? This problem is that of the filing order between collateral classes, and it is decided on the basis of the principle of inversion; that is, we must choose the citation order between the four sub-facets, and file them in the reverse order—assuming that we want to have broader-narrower order between documents on our shelves, or records of documents in our classified catalogue. It is possible with a faceted scheme using a certain kind of notation to leave this decision to the classifier using our scheme, but we shall make it now.

The citation order decision is the choice of collocation for a work which could be placed in more than one class; for example, a work on Land Animals of Tropical Wooded

Coasts could be placed in each of our four subfacets. Which subfacet is to have its documents collocated? In the case of superimposed classes, such as we are now dealing with, the guides to choice of citation order are not very helpful—as all the classes are kinds of the same thing, none can be more concrete than others; and none can be regarded as the purpose or end product of the study more than others. Perhaps consensus might help: do students of zoology usually study animals defined by element, rather than animals defined by latitude? No, there is no guidance there. Let us take examples, and see whether we have any preferences. Suppose we had a work on the class ANIMALS OF THE TROPICAL WOODLANDS, would we rather keep this with Tropical Animals or Woodland Animals? Put like that, latitude seems to be a more fundamental characteristic than ground cover; this is an unsatisfactory basis for a decision, but we have no better one; so let us decide to cite 'by latitude' before 'by ground cover'. Now, consider a work on TROPICAL FRESH WATER ANIMALS; shall we collocate this with other works on tropical animals, or other works on fresh water animals? Again, intuition suggests that 'by element' should be preferred to 'by latitude'; so we now have the citation order element—latitude—ground cover, and we only have to fit in 'by land form'.

Take a work on Animals of Mountain Rivers—let us keep it with RIVER ANIMALS; Tropical Mountain Animals? —keep it with TROPICAL ANIMALS; what about a work with the title *Animals of the High Grasslands?*—again, let us prefer GRASSLAND ANIMALS to UPLAND ANIMALS. These decisions, admittedly made without firm intellectual bases, as seems to be inevitable when choosing citation order for superimposed classes, have given us the citation order by element—by latitude—by ground cover—by land form; and we shall, therefore, file our four subfacets in the order by land form—by ground cover—by latitude—by element. This results in the following final organisation of foci in the 'animals by habitat' subfacet:

(Animals by habitat)
  (by land form)
    Coastal animals
      Littoral animals/Animals of the sea shore
    Lowland animals
    Upland animals
      Hill animals
      Mountain animals
  (by ground cover)
    Desert animals
    Grassland animals
    Scrubland animals
    Woodland animals
      Jungle animals
  (by latitude)
    Polar animals
    Temperate animals
    Tropical animals
      Equatorial animals
  (by element)
    Aquatic/Water animals
      Fresh water animals
        River animals
        Lake animals
      Marine/Sea/Salt water animals
    Amphibious animals
    Land animals

The elemental classes which made up our example Land Animals of Tropical Wooded Coasts would be assembled in the order: LAND ANIMALS–TROPICAL ANIMALS –WOODLAND ANIMALS–COASTAL ANIMALS. This document would file after any document on a broader class; it would file after LAND ANIMALS–TROPICAL ANIMALS–WOODLAND ANIMALS, and TROPICAL ANIMALS–WOODLAND ANIMALS–COASTAL ANIMALS, and WOODLAND ANIMALS–COASTAL ANIMALS and so on, because we have followed the principle of inversion.

Carrying out the same operations on the other subfacets in the Animals facet, we would get the following:

(Animals by effect on man subfacet)
  Beneficial animals
  Harmful animals
    Venomous animals

(Animals by habit subfacet)
  Hibernating animals
  Migratory animals

(this order in array was chosen on the assumption that hibernation is a more primitive reaction to changing conditions than migraion)

(Animals by zoologists' taxonomy subfacet)
  Invertebrates
    Arachnids
      Spiders
    Insects
      Lepidoptera
        Moths
          Leaf moths
        Butterflies
      Hymenoptera
        Bees
          Honeybees

  Vertebrates
    Fish
    Amphibians
      Frogs
      Toads
    Reptiles
      Lizards
      Snakes
      Tortoises
    Birds
      Raptors/Birds of prey
        Eagles
          Golden eagles

                Mammals
                    Rodents
                        Rats
                    Procyonidae
                        Pandas
                    Bears
                        Pandas
                    Primates
                        Monkeys
                            Colobus monkeys
                        Man

(The orders in array in this subfacet more or less follow those which zoologists would use, and are mostly based on developmental order—eg INVERTEBRATES—VERTEBRATES; FISH—AMPHIBIANS—REPTILES—BIRDS—MAMMALS.)

Our last decision in the animals facet is the choice of filing order between the subfacets habitat, effect on man, habit and zoologists' taxonomy. We shall file them in the reverse of their citation order, and this is easier to choose now, because at least the different subfacets are based on completely different characteristics. Let us assume the citation order zoologists' taxonomy—habitat—habit—effect on man (but remembering that in different situations different orders could be appropriate—for example, if most of our clients were interested in economic zoology then the 'animals by effect on man' subfacet would be cited first); this gives the filing order effect on man—habit—habitat—zoologists' taxonomy. As we will shortly be showing the whole scheme, we shall not illustrate the result of the decision here; in any case, it should be quite clear.

Having organised the foci in the Animals facet we can treat the other facets in the same way, although none of them has the complication of subfacets. We are then faced with one final decision—the choice of filing order between facets. Foci in different facets are collateral classes of the first type—they are different kinds of things (animals, processes, operations etc). The filing order of facets should, therefore, be the reverse of the citation order for compound classes, if we want to have broader-narrower order between documents or records of documents. Again, for faceted schemes, a special kind of notation may be provided which allows the classifier using the scheme to make the decision (it is more usual to do this for facets than for subfacets); but we shall do so now.

It seems likely that all three guides to choice of citation order—decreasing concreteness, purpose and, perhaps, consensus—indicate the same primary facet: Animals. Consensus certainly suggests Physiological processes and parts as the secondary facet. As Activities (such as PLAY) depend on Attributes (such as INTELLIGENCE) as well as Physiological processes, perhaps we should cite Attributes after Physiological processes and Activities after Attributes. The general processes facet, whose foci are DEVELOPMENT/MATURATION and ADAPTATION, should come next. This leaves the Operations facet to follow; and lastly the Form facet, which in parts of schemes based on the subjects of documents must always be cited last. This citation order (Animals—Physiological processes—Attributes—Activities—General processes—Operations—Form) gives the filing order Form—Operations—General processes—Activities—Attributes—Physiological processes—Animals. We can now write out the complete set of classes in order—our classification schedule:

Zoology
  (Form of presentation facet)
      Essays
      Periodicals
  (Operations facet)
    Collection
    Experiments
      Field experiments
      Laboratory experiments
    Identification
      Classification/Taxonomy (we can still insert new
                      synonyms)
      Naming/Nomenclature
  (General processes facet)
    Development/Maturation
    Adaptation

(Activities facet)
  Activities/Behaviour (it is obvious that names of facets
    Social behaviour need not also appear as foci; in this
      Play   case it is necessary)
    Hibernation
    Migration
(Attributes facet)
  Intelligence
  Aggression
(Physiological processes and parts facet)
  Anatomy
  (nb particular parts are enumerated under their function
  or system below)
  Physiology
    Skin
    Nervour system
      Brain
      Senses
        Sight/Visual system
      Respiration/Breathing
      Nutrition/Feeding
      Locomotion
        Running
        Flying
      Reproduction
(Animals facet)
  Animals/Fauna
    (by effect on man subfacet)
      Beneficial animals
      Harmful animals
        Venomous/Poisonous animals
    (by habit subfacet)
      Hibernating animals
      Migratory animals
    (by habitat subfacet)
      (by land form)
        Coastal animals
          Littoral fauna/Animals of the sea shore
        Lowland animals
        Upland animals

(Animal facet)
    (by habitat subfacet)
      (by land form) continued
        Hill animals
        Mountain animals
      (by ground cover)
        Desert animals
        Grassland animals
        Scrubland animals
        Woodland/Forest animals
          Jungle animals
      (by latitude)
        Polar animals
        Temperate zone animals
        Tropical animals
          Equatorial animals
      (by element)
        Aquatic/Water animals
          Fresh water animals
            River animals
            Lake animals
          Marine/Sea/Salt water animals
        Amphibious animals
        Land animals
    (by zoologists' taxonomy subfacet)
      Invertebrates
      Arachnids
        Spiders
      Insects
        Lepidoptera
          Moths
            Leaf moths
          Butterflies
        Hymenoptera
          Bees
            Honeybees
      Vertebrates
      Fish
      Amphibians
        Frogs
        Toads

(Animal facet)
    (by zoologists' taxonomy subfacet)
      Vertebrates continued
        Reptiles
          Lizards
          Snakes
          Tortoises
        Birds
          Raptors/Birds of prey
            Eagles
              Golden Eagles
        Mammals
          Rodents
            Rats
          Procyonidae
            Pandas
          Bears
            Pandas
          Primates
            Monkeys
              Colobus monkeys
            Man

SEVEN

NOTATION: I

AS WE indicated in our previous chapter we have now done enough. We have created a tool which can be used to organise a collection of documents on Zoology, grouping them in a preferred collocation and filing them in helpful order. With our scheme we could classify all of the titles on which it was based.

However, to apply our scheme, we should have to remember the filing order between all the classes—or constantly check it by referring to the scheme—and so should the library staff who are shelving documents, or arranging entries in a catalogue. This is not very practical, especially when dealing with documents on superimposed or composite classes composed of several elemental classes; but it is possible. What is much more difficult is to explain to a client the location of documents on a given subject. In order to tell him where he could find information on, say, Experiments in the Physiology of Vertebrates, we should have to rehearse the whole systematic order of documents to him. The problem is that, although the order which results from the application of our scheme is helpful, it is not, and cannot be, simple—as alphabetical order by author's name is, for example.

This problem was realised by Thomas Jefferson, President of the United States. He has been called 'the compleat gentlemen of the eighteenth century, planter, scholar, inventor, expert or dabbler in every art and science'(1), and, like other polymaths of the time (including his colleague, Benjamin Franklin) he compiled a classification scheme. This was for use in his library at Monticello, the Palladian villa which, naturally, he designed himself. Jefferson's scheme, owing much to that of Francis Bacon, was in one

71

way something like ours in its present state: it produced a helpful collocation and order, but the order was not obvious. This is clear from the following excerpt from a letter to James Ogilvie, written by Jefferson and dated from Monticello, 31st January 1806:

'... the key is at present in the hands of mr Dinsmore, at [Monticello], who on sight of this letter will consider you as at all times authorised to have access to the library ... the arrangement is as follows. 1 Antient history. 2 Modern do. 3 Physics. 4 Nat. hist. proper. 5 Technical arts. 6 Ethics. 7 Jurisprudence. 8 Mathematics. 9 Gardening, architecture, sculpture, painting, music. 9 [sic] Poetry. 10 Oratory. 11 Criticism. 12 Polygraphy. you will find this on a paper nailed up somewhere in the library ... as after using a book, you may be at a loss in returning it to it's exact place, & they cannot be found again when misplaced, it will be better to leave them on a table in the room. my familiarity with their place will enable me to replace them readily ...'(2)

Jefferson's library was later 'ceded to Congress to replace the devastation of British vandalism at Washington'(3), as the foundation of the revived Library of Congress (destroyed by 'British vandalism' during the 1812 war). By that time Jefferson had solved the problem; in a letter from Monticello, dated 7th May 1815, he tells the newly-appointed Librarian of Congress, George Watterston, that:

'on every book is a label, indicating the chapter of the catalogue to which it belongs, and the order it holds among those of the same format.'(4)

That is, each book had been given an address, in the form of a symbol which has an obvious filing value in a sequence of similar symbols, and which was based on the symbol for the class from his scheme to which the book had been assigned. (We might note that, nearly 150 years earlier, Samuel Pepys also gave his books labels on which their addresses were written, although as his library was not in systematic order these addresses were shelf-marks—in the form of arabic numerals—rather than symbols for subject classes. On 19th December 1666, after a particularly worrying day, he writes:

'Home, full of trouble on these considerations. And among other things, I to my chamber and there to ticket a good part of my books, in order to the Numbring of them—for my easy finding them to read, as I have occasion. So to supper and to bed—with my heart full of trouble.'(5))

If we add symbols of this kind—which we call 'notation'— to our scheme, we shall be able to give each document an address which will show its filing position, and make the filing and finding of documents easy; we can express combinations of elemental classes by joining their notations together; and we can link our alphabetical index to the list of classes efficiently, by using notation. We shall consider below other advantages which notation brings; but perhaps we had better reiterate here that notation cannot be considered essential to a classification scheme (the library of the Royal Geographical Society still has what amounts to a classified catalogue in which entries are filed—and found— without benefit of notation), and that it is used to show what our preferred order is and not to determine that order. As Bliss says, it is 'subsidiary'(6)—and we should add it after we made the decisions about collocation and order we have discussed.

Because for most people the notation IS the classification scheme, while we know that it is only a relatively unimportant part of the scheme, there has been a tendency, perhaps, to under-emphasise notation in textbooks and lecture programmes. We have to acknowledge that the acceptability of a scheme to our clients depends very largely on the qualities of its notation—especially its ease of use— and schemes in which all the decisions about collocation and order have been made with care may still fail because of their notation. This is true even when the clients are themselves librarians—the College of Librarianship Wales abandoned, in its library, the very good faceted scheme for librarianship (CLIS) developed by the Classification Research Group, in favour of the inferior DC because of the complexity of notation of the former. Lecturers have tended to use Bliss's famous statement on this subject to reinforce the point that notation is not all-important; perhaps we should give more weight to the last four words:

'Librarians have been so accustomed to seeing the notation come first in the schedules and on catalog-cards that they are prone to think of notation as the thing of first importance;

73

but the truth is that the classification is the main thing, and that the notation, however real its service, does not make the classification, tho it may mar it'.(7)

If we are to avoid marring our scheme, then, we must consider the properties and qualities of notation carefully. These fall into two groups: those which affect the ease of use of the notation, and those which ensure that any class which the scheme may have to accommodate may be given a unique notation. The decisions we must make in the first group are these: what sets of symbols to use; how long is notation to be; is the notation to be hierarchical; is it to be mnemonic; and shall we allow alternative locations for the same class. Some of our choices will have conflicting results: for example, as we shall see, if we choose to have hierarchical notation we cannot also choose another desirable quality, brevity.

Notation must be based on numerals or letters or both, because these are the only sets of symbols with a generally accepted and known order. Of the two, numerals may display order more obviously, especially as it has become less common for the alphabet to be taught by rote in schools (compare these two notations for the same class—the first from BC, the second from DC: HKG and 796.334; which do you think is easier used as an address?).

If we use one set of symbols only, then we have pure notation; its advantage over mixed notation, which uses more than one set, is that users do not have to learn the filing value of the different sets—for example, which files first, a letter or a numeral?—and besides, mixed notation looks more complicated. Mixed notation may consist of any combination of numerals, upper case letters and lower case letters; and it may even include symbols with no obvious ordinal value (eg : ; ( )). The effect of this may be gauged by comparing the two notations in each of the following pairs—they represent the same class:

1 Elizabethan England   DA355 (LC) 942.055 (DC)
2 Women's colleges   376.8 (DC) SabRag (LEC)
3 Elizabethan drama   822.3 (DC) 820-2"1558/1603"
                                                  (UDC)

It is pleasant to be able to say something nice about DC; these examples show quite convincingly the ease of use which its notational simplicity brings—perhaps its one clear advantage over other schemes. But as we shall see, mixed notation, even with symbols with no accepted filing value, has its uses.

One of the irritations of mixed notation is that we may have to distinguish between the different sets in speech (eg, we might have to say 'lower case a' and 'upper case A'); to name the symbols if we are using those with no ordinal value (eg '820 hyphen 2 inverted commas 1558-1603'); and to write with care (so as to distinguish between 0 and O, or between 1, I and l, for example).

One advantage of mixed notation is that it gives a longer base for the notation; that is, it provides more symbols for use than does a pure notation. If we use the alphabet alone, in upper case, we have twenty-six symbols to play with; if we use numerals alone we have ten; but if we use both sets then we have thirty-six, and more if we include lower case letters and arbitrary symbols. The benefit of a longer base if that it tends to give shorter notations for classes, and brevity in notation is an aid to ease of use (Bliss thought that 'the economic limit' for class notation is three or four digits (8)).

Suppose we had only twenty classes in our scheme, and used upper case letters for our notation, then no class need have more than one letter for its notation because there are twenty-six letters. If we used numerals alone, then we should have a shorter base of only ten different symbols, 0-9; and half of our classes would have to be given notation with more than one digit. This is a good example of the conflict which a quality or property may bring: mixed notation may produce more complicated notations than pure notation (which is unhelpful) but it also tends to produce briefer notations (which is helpful).

One of the other causes of long notation is poor allocation of spans of symbols, so that some parts of the scheme are given a disproportionately large share of the notational base. This may be due to carelessness by the compiler, or it may be that after the completion of the structure of the scheme some areas of knowledge expanded, producing many new subclasses, while others stagnated; so that what was originally a fair share of notation is no longer so. DC provides many good (or bad) examples. In DC18, LOGIC and its subclasses is allocated the span of numbers from 160 to 169; while ELECTRICAL ENGINEERING and its subclasses is allowed only 621.3 and its subdivisions. As there are only seven subclasses in Logic in this scheme, none of them has a notation longer than three digits, which is DC's minimum (eg SYLLOGISMS 166); but there are over 300 subordinate classes in Electrical engineering, with the result that very few of them have notations less than twice as long as those in Logic. Indeed, many have notations more than three times as long (eg DIODES 621.381 512 2), and some have four times as many digits (eg TRANSISTORISED CIRCUITS 621.381 530 422)—and these cumbersome notations occur in a part of a general library which tends to be much more heavily used than the Logic section.

The DC examples illustrate two further points about brevity. One is that the imposition of a minimum length shortens the base—DC has a three figure minimum, so that notations such as 6 or 62 may not be used, and these symbols are wasted (UDC, which was derived from DC and whose notation is basically similar, does not impose a minimum); the other is that very long notations may be made easier to use by being broken up into groups, either by punctuation or spacing. As you can see, DC uses both; BC2 uses only spacing, as in JHS LOP DQN (which is the notation for the superimposed class ENGAGED FEMALE TEACHER-LIBRARIANS). Other properties which affect the brevity of notation are mentioned below.

If the notation displays the relationship of subordination by adding a new symbol for each successively subordinate class, it is said to be hierarchical. This example is from CC:

D5	Vehicles
D51	Land vehicles
D515	Railway vehicles
D5153	Railway carriages
D51533	Passenger carriages
D515332	Higher class passenger carriages

This kind of notation may be said to be structural, because it displays part of the structure of the scheme (the other kind of structural notation is expressive notation, dealt with in the next chapter; we might say that hierarchical notation displays the generic structure, while expressive notation displays syntactical structure). Hierarchical notation tends to be longer than ordinal (that is, non-hierarchical) notation, but it makes systematic browsing easier—this is another example of a notational property which is both beneficial and harmful, and the two must be balanced before we decide to make our notation hierarchical. (Incidentally, the name 'ordinal' should not be allowed to mislead you—of course hierarchical notation also shows order; but ordinal notation *merely* shows order, and does not display subordinate relationships as well.) Consider the following two examples; the notation on the left is hierarchical (from DC), while that on the right is ordinal (from BC1):

796.3	Ball games	HKE	Ball games
796.33	Football	HKF	Football
796.333	Rugby	HKG	Soccer
796.334	Soccer	HKH	Hockey
796.34	Racket games	HKI	Polo
796.342	Tennis	HKJ	Lacrosse

The advantage of brevity in the ordinal notation is obvious; but the hierarchical notation is more satisfying because it makes the structure so clear, and many clients do find ordinal notation less acceptable—especially when, as sometimes happens in BC2, subordinate classes have longer notations than their parent classes:

JKG	Mother tongue
JKG Y	Reading and writing
JKH	Reading

or the notation seems to imply a subordination which is not there:

JHN	Female teachers
JHN P	Male teachers

However, the real advantage of hierarchical notation is that it helps us to broaden and narrower searches more easily. Suppose we were looking for information on Soccer and

77

found nothing at 796.334; we know there is no point in looking at 796.333, or 796.332, because the hierarchical notation tells us that these classes are coordinate with SOCCER, and we need to go to the next superordinate class— the class whose notation contains one digit less than the notation we originally searched for. Because this class is broader than that we are seeking, documents on it ought to give information about our class—that is, works on the class FOOTBALL should contain information on all kinds of football including Soccer; but there is no reason why a work on a coordinate class such as RUGBY should give us information about Soccer.

This facility of hierarchical notation is important when a scheme is used as the basis for the organisation of machine-readable records. Because computers are not intelligent, they are not able to broaden or narrow searches unless the labels given to records explicitly state their superordinate-subordinate relationship; if the labels are notation from a classification scheme, therefore, the notation must be hierarchical.(9) For the same reason when, in the 1950s, the Commonwealth Plant Breeding Bureau at Cambridge tried a primitive form of mechanisation using punched cards with UDC notation as the index language, the notation had to be adapted to make it absolutely hierarchical (and also to make sure that the same concept always had the same notation, which was not the case with the unadapted UDC because it was not properly faceted)(10). Still, the tendency in modern special schemes has been to make the notation ordinal, for brevity; and also because, as we shall see in the next chapter, hierarchical notation is difficult to reconcile with hospitality.

Memorability of notation is of minor importance—after all, notations can always be written down. Still, if it can be achieved it will be one more advantage. If our scheme uses synthesis (as a faceted scheme does; but so do most basically enumerative schemes, to some extent) then the same symbols will always represent the same concept, whatever context it appears in. These symbols, therefore, become easily associated with that concept, and are memorable. Mnemonics of this kind are called 'systematic mnemonics', because they derive from the structure of the scheme. Here is a simple example from DC18; it does not involve synthesis, although clearly faceted principles were in the mind of the compiler:

811 American poetry	821 English poetry	831 German poetry
812 American drama	822 English drama	832 German drama
813 American fiction	823 English fiction	833 German fiction
814 American essays	824 English essays	824 German essays

It is not difficult to deduce from this set of classes, nor to remember, that, for example, − − 1 means Poetry, and − − 4 means Essays (at least in the class LITERATURE— in other main classes they will mean something quite different).

Alphabetical notations allow two other kinds of mnemonic. The first is called 'literal mnemonics', which are notational symbols which could stand for the name of the class in ordinary language. For example, in BC the class CHEMISTRY has the notation C, and AGRICULTURE (which is a subclass of USEFUL ARTS) the notation UA; similarly, in LC the class TECHNOLOGY has the notation T. Of course, the order of classes must not be tampered with to achieve literal mnemonics—notation is added after such decisions are made, so that Chemistry must not be given the symbol C unless it is appropriate to the filing order of the class. Perhaps we had better also say that notation is not a short-hand form of the name of the subject(11), as literal mnemonics might tempt us to suppose. (A personal anecdote, which provides a pleasing example of this false belief: earlier this year I gave our Departmental secretary a handout to type; she commented, sourly, that indexing lecturers always made simple things seem difficult. Piqued, I challenged her to give an example, and she produced a book on library management which bore the notation ZQF—our college library uses BC—and demanded to know why it could not be given the notation Lib Man; what had ZQF to do with library management? I gave up the argument, merely suggesting that she should attend some of our lectures.)

The second kind of memorable alphabetical notation was first put forward by Cordonnier(12). It is called 'syllabic notation', in which consonants and vowels are so arranged that notations are pronounceable; and, therefore, easily remembered. An extension of pronounceable notation might be called 'suggestive mnemonics'—some examples from LEC will make the meaning clear: in this scheme the class CHOIR SCHOOLS has the notation Ror; OUTWARD BOUND SCHOOLS has the notation Ruf; EXAMINATIONS is Jib; and TEACHING STAFF is, of course, Fab. We need to be careful to avoid unfortunate combinations of letters when designing alphabetical notations, and expecially so when the result is meant to be pronounced—after all, delicately-nurtured clients will not find the notation easy to use if they are forced to write, or worse, to say, combinations of letters which look or sound like words not normally used in polite society. This is easy enough to do for our enumerated elemental classes; but synthesis might produce some surprising combinations.

REFERENCES

1 Sinclair, Andrew *Concise history of the United States* Thames & Hudson, 1967.

2 to be found in, for example La Montagne, Leo E *American library classification* Hamden (Conn), Shoe String Press, 1961.

3 Ibid.

4 Ibid.

5 Pepys, Samuel *Diary*; edited by Robert Latham & William Matthews. vol 7, Bell, 1972.

6 Bliss, Henry Evelyn *Organization of knowledge in libraries* 2nd ed, New York, Wilson, 1939.

7 Ibid.

8 Ibid.

9 Schneider, John H 'Modern classification' *Drexel library quarterly*, 10 (4) October 1974.

10 reported in Casey, R S (et al) *Punched cards* 2nd ed, New York, Reinhardt; London, Chapman & Hall, 1958.

11 Bliss, op cit.

12 Foskett, D J *Classification and indexing in the social sciences* Butterworths, 1963.

EIGHT

NOTATION: II

LIBRARIANS who use our scheme will want to collocate documents in the way which is most helpful to their clients, and this may vary from library to library. It is reasonable for us to attempt to provide alternative locations—or the possibility of alternative locations—for classes in our scheme, to satisfy these different needs. Bliss says:

'Classifications are relative and adaptive, and systems should, as far as is feasible, serve various tho not incompatible interests. Alternative locations should therefore be provided . . .'(1)

Schemes which provide for different collocations may be said to be 'flexible'; flexibility is provided through the scheme's notation. There are two methods of achieving flexibility: one is to reserve different notations (in different contexts) for the same class; the second is to allow the classifier using the scheme to choose his own citation order. We may take examples from BC2, as a tribute to Bliss's concern for this quality. The first method is shown by the classes PHYSICS BASED TECHNOLOGIES and MATERIALS SCIENCE AND TECHNOLOGY. The first class has two notations reserved for it, one—BR—in the context of Science, the other—UG—in the context of Technology; similarly, the second may be placed with Chemistry in CT or with Technology in UEV. Of course, once a particular library has chosen one of these locations it can never use the other, and the notation reserved there remains unused and wasted.

If we want to allow the classifier to choose his citation order we must enable him to change the filing order between facets or subfacets, so that whatever citation order he adopts, the filing order of documents will still be broader-narrower.

This can be done, again, by reserving different notations for the same facet or subfacet (which will lead to a waste of notation, as above); or we may give the notations for use in facets and subfacets introductory symbols whose filing value can be changed—that is, symbols with no accepted filing value, so that whatever filing value is assigned to them is necessarily of local value only. This second technique is discussed below under 'facet indicators'. The first technique is used in BC2, as in this example from the class Education:

JI	Teaching methods and aids facet
JK	Curriculum facet
JL/JV	Educands facet
JW	Teaching methods and aids facet
JY	Curriculum facet

Bearing in mind the principle of inversion, we can see that this gives the classifier a choice of two citation orders: either Educands—Curriculum—Teaching methods or Curriculum—Teaching methods—Educands. This is a reasonable choice—I once worked in a college library whose education section was used by people who knew which curriculum subjects they wanted to teach, but who had not decided at what level they were going to teach; for these clients the second citation order would have been better, but unfortunately the scheme we were using had the first citation order, and it was inflexible. Now, if our classifier chooses the first citation order he wants the filing order of the facets to be Teaching methods—Curriculum—Educands, so he will use the notations

JI	Teaching methods and aids facet
JK	Curriculum facet
JL/JV	Educands facet

and leave JW and JY unused. If he prefers the other citation order, then the filing order of facets must be changed to Educands—Teaching methods—Curriculum, in order to give broader-narrower shelf order, and he will use the notations

JL/JV	Educands facet
JW	Teaching methods and aids facet
JY	Curriculum facet

and the notations JI and JK will be wasted.

Our scheme must be able to give a unique notation to any class it may have to accommodate, whether elemental, superimposed or composite, and including new classes which had not been discovered at the time the scheme was compiled. One of the problems in this area is to avoid the possibility of a synthesised notation duplicating the notation for an enumerated class. For example, in the Materials facet of CLIS we find the class ILLUSTRATIONS, with its notation OD. Later, in the Operations facet, we find SUBJECT INDEXING, for which the notation is W, and a subordinate class ORDER, ARRANGEMENT whose notation is WOD. As is stands, the notation for the compound class SUBJECT INDEXING OF ILLUSTRATIONS will be WOD—that is, W + OD (following the principle of inversion, classes which file later should be cited first). Unfortunately, we now have the same notation representing two quite different classes. To avoid this inefficiency we have to differentiate enumerated from synthesised notation; that is, in the context of our faceted scheme, we must display the fact that we are expressing a syntactical relationship, as opposed to merely giving a notation for an elemental class. Notation which does this is called 'expressive'. Expressive notation is a kind of structural notation (the other kind is hierarchical notation, already discussed, which displays generic structure; you will find confusion over these terms in most textbooks, which tend to use them indiscriminately). Apart from avoiding ambiguity, expressiveness ensures that synthetic notation files in the right place (for example, the class SUBJECT INDEXING OF ILLUSTRATIONS should file after SUBJECT INDEXING but before ORDER, which is an enumerated subclass of SUBJECT INDEXING; but of course, our two identical notations, WOD and WOD, do not allow this to happen, because we have not yet made the notation expressive'. It may also release symbols for re-use with a different meaning elsewhere (for example, using CC the notation for the class CASTING BRONZE EQUESTRIAN FIGURES is ND,11;5;5 in which the first 5 means Bronze, but the second means Casting; the meanings are differentiated by the punctuation marks attached to the numerals, which make the notation expressive).

The first and simplest kind of expressive notation inserts a symbol between the elements of synthesised notation. This symbol is called a 'fence' (although in BC2, which sometimes uses this device, it is called an 'intercalator').

A fence must have a filing value less than that of any symbol used in the representation of a class, so that the synthesised notation shall file immediately after the notation for the elemental class which precedes the fence; for example, CLIS uses / as a fence, and this gives the following order for our examples above:

W   Subject indexing
W/OD   Subject indexing of illustrations
WOD   Order, arrangement

If we would prefer a pure notation then we can reserve the first symbol of the set we are using for class notation as the fence; BC2 does this, and as its notation consists of upper case letters its fence is the symbol A. For example, here are two enumerated classes from the class Education:

JH   Teaching and teachers
JHE B   Hours of teachers

Now, the class EVALUATION OF TEACHERS is not enumerated; its notation must be synthesised from JEB, which means EVALUATION in an earlier sequence, and JH. Of course, we shall cite JH first—as it files later we must do, by the principle of inversion—and then we can add JEB, first knocking off the J which simply stands for Education and is already present in JH. This gives us the notation JHE B; which is the same as the notation for the enumerated class HOURS OF TEACHERS. We are, therefore, instructed to insert the fence A between the elements of synthesised notation, giving the notation JHA EB, and the filing sequence

JH   Teaching and teachers
JHA EB   Evaluation of teachers
JHE B   Hours of teachers

If we are prepared to accept mixed notation then we can produce expressiveness by the use of facet indicators. These are symbols from a different set to that used for the subject subdivisions of the scheme; each facet (and, if required, each subfacet) is given its own facet indicator, which is used to introduce any notation from that facet (or subfacet). Synthesised notation is then differentiated from enumerated notation by the appearance of symbols of a different set within the notation for the class; these symbols have a filing value less than that of the main set, so that synthesised notation files in the right place; and the main set symbols may be used again and again in different facets, as the facet indicators give a unique combination of symbols for any class. In LEC the main set of symbols consists of lower case letters; the facet indicators are upper case letters—eg R introduces the Educands facet. In the Educands facet we find notations such as Rav, for the class PRIMARY SCHOOLS; in the Curriculum facet Men, which stands for FOREIGN LANGUAGES; and in Teaching methods, Lep, which represents GROUP TEACHING. If we synthesise these to accommodate the compound class GROUP TEACHING OF FOREIGN LANGUAGES IN PRIMARY SCHOOLS we get the notation RavMenLep, which is clearly synthetic.

Provided that it differs from the main set we may use any set of symbols for facet indicators, including arbitrary symbols—those with no accepted filing value. Arbitrary symbols—punctuation marks, mathematical symbols etc—make the notation more complex and difficult to use; but because they have no accepted filing value, we may impose any value that we like; and this makes flexibility through choice of citation order much easier. If we use letters or numbers as facet indicators, we cannot change the filing order of the facets to fit in with a changed citation order without re-designing the whole notation—we cannot say to our clients 'In this library you will find that we file 4 after 7' or 'I'm afraid that in this library H comes before D', because the filing values of these symbols are too well established. If our facet indicators are symbols such as ; : = or ( ), then that problem does not exist. It will be just as easy (or just as difficult) for our clients to accept that : files before ; as to accept that ; files before : .

An example from UDC will illustrate the use of arbitrary symbols in this way. As we said earlier, UDC's class Literature is faceted, and in what we would call the Literary works facet we can discern three subfacets—Works by period, Works by form and Works by language. It is assumed that the Language subfacet will be cited first, and symbols for language are added immediately on to the notation 8, which represents Literature:

820 English literature
830 German literature
840 French literature
850 Italian literature
etc

The other two subfacets are given facet indicators in the form of punctuation marks:

−1	Poetry	"17"	18th century literature
−2	Drama	"18"	19th century literature
−3	Prose	"19"	20th century literature
−4	Novels	"1939/1945"	Literature of the Second World War
etc		etc	

Let us classify six works by this scheme, using two different citation orders.

	Language− Period−Form	Language− Form−Period
19th century English literature	820"18"	820"18"
The English novel	820−31	820−31
19th century English drama	820"18"−2	820−2"18"
English literature	820	820
19th century English novel	820"18"−31	820−31"18"
English drama	820−2	820−2

When we come to place these sets in order, we must make − file before " " for the Language−Period−Form citation order, but " " file before − for the Language−Form−Period citation order; thus

820	820
820−2	820"18"
820−31	820−2
820"18"	820−2"18"
820"18"−2	820−31
820"18"−31	820−31"18"

The third method of achieving expressiveness is through the use of 'retroactive notation'. Here is a simple model, based on three facets from a possible classification scheme for Librarianship; the citation order is Libraries—Materials—Operations:

D	Library operations
DE	Acquisition
DF	Indexing
DFE	Subject indexing
DG	Circulation

E	Library materials
EF	Print materials
EFE	Books
EFF	Periodicals
EG	Non-print materials
EGE	Audio-visual materials
EGEF	Audio materials
EGEG	Visual materials

F	Libraries
FG	Public libraries
FH	Academic libraries
FI	Special libraries

The principles of this technique are that the facets are filed in the reverse of their citation order (the principle of inversion has been observed); each facet is given an introductory symbol from the same set as that used for foci; within each facet, no symbol is used in the notation for a focus which has a filing value less than that of that facet's introductory symbol—for example, for foci in the Materials facet the letters A, B, C and D may not be used; in the Libraries facet A, B, C, D and E may not be used. The name 'retroactive notation' is not very helpful. It merely means that, in synthesising, one takes the notation for the focus in the facet which files latest, and 'works backward' towards the beginning of the scheme, adding notations as necessary. For example, the notation for the class SUBJECT INDEXING OF NON-PRINT MEDIA IN SPECIAL LIBRARIES is FHEGDFE—but this happens whenever facets are filed in the reverse of citation order, whatever the kind of notation.

Retroactive notation is pure, and gives expressiveness without the need for additional symbols such as a fence or facet indicators: it is not possible to produce a synthetic notation which duplicates that for an enumerated class; the filing order of classes expressed by synthesis is correct; and, with the exception which is the basis of the technique, symbols may be re-used in other facets. However, retroactive notation does not give flexibility, and the base becomes shorter the nearer one moves towards the primary facet—with a numerical notation, which already has a short base, this may be unacceptable: by the time facet 8 is reached, only the digits 8 and 9 may be used. For this reason this form of notation tends to be used with letters, as it is in BC2—the major example of a scheme with retroactive notation.

The ability of our scheme to give a unique code to any class it may have to accommodate, means that it must be able to accept new classes which had not been discovered when it was compiled. Schemes whose notations allows the precise specification of new classes in their correct filing order are said to be hospitable; this excludes schemes which include a class labelled OTHER, in which any new class may be placed—for example, by our definition this sequence from DC18 is not hospitable:

787.5   Harp
787.6   Guitar
787.7   Banjo
787.8   Zither
787.9   Other plectral instruments

It is usual to distinguish two kinds of hospitality, called 'hospitality in array' (that is hospitality to new coordinate classes) and 'hospitality in chain' (that is to new subordinate classes, or new combinations of classes)(2). These concepts seem not to be very helpful, because the only problem that we have is that of providing a place for a new elemental class—provided the notation is expressive, as it must be to be efficient, our scheme will automatically be hospitable to any new combination of elemental classes. Even if we were constructing an enumerative scheme the distinction is unnecessary, because both hospitality in chain and hospitality in array are provided by the same quality of notation: that any existing notation should be divisible. This same quality is the only positive one needed to make our faceted scheme hospitable to new elemental classes.

Notation which is not divisible is called, rather unhelpfully, 'arithmetical', even when it is based on letters; but then the thing itself seems wilfully unhelpful. Consider this sequence from LEC1, whose notation consists of an upper case letter followed by two lower case letters, and which we are not allowed to extend (or divide):

Tig	Slow learning
Tik	Retarded
Til	Illiterate
Tim	Malajusted

Suppose we now wish to insert the new class NON-READERS. This class is obviously subordinate to ILLITERATE, and should follow that class; but there is no way in which we can give it notation which will make it file there—there is no notation between Til and Tim. It is true that we can place it at, say, Tij, where a gap has been left; but gap notation is obviously inefficient—gaps get left in the wrong place, as here, so that the notation actually distorts the order when we know it should merely reflect it. Besides, what happens when all the gaps get filled? (What happens in LC, which uses gap notation, is that when there are no more gaps one is allowed to divide existing notation—AFTER the misplacing has been accomplished!)

All that we need to be able to do is to divide an existing notation and the problem would disappear—to be able to give the class NON-READERS the notation Tile, say, would make the scheme truly hospitable. (Incidentally, the reason why LEC1 had an arithmetical notation was probably to retain the neatness of three letters per enumerated class, and to ensure that the notation remained syllabic—it is a good example of the need for us to be aware of the relative importance of the different qualities of notation).

Given divisible notation (sometimes called fractional or decimal notation), then our scheme can accommodate any new classes in the right places. In doing this, however, we may be forced to abandon the attempt to make our notation hierarchical. Consider this sequence of selected classes, in which the chain is complete although not all coordinate classes have been included (the sequence is from DC18):

700	Arts	
704	General special aspects of fine arts	
704.9	Iconography and collections of writings	
704.92	Collections of writings	
704.94	Iconography (that is, the study of subjects of art)	
704.942	Human figures	
704.943	Nature and still life	
704.9432	Animals	
704.9435	Still life	
704.9436	Landscape	
704.9437	Marine scenes	

It seems perfectly feasible that the class SCENERY might occur, which is superordinate to LANDSCAPE and MARINE SCENES, and subordinate to NATURE AND STILL LIFE. This new class should file between 704.9435 and 704.9436 —say, at 704.94358. This is a perfectly good notation, but it is not hierarchical; to be so its needs to be one digit longer than the notation for NATURE AND STILL LIFE, and one digit shorter than that for LANDSCAPE—which is not possible. Further, the new notation seems to imply that SCENERY is subordinate to STILL LIFE; as this is not so, the notation is not hierarchical. When we have this sort of conflict between hospitality and hierarchical notation we must prefer hospitality.

Another aspect of the conflict between hospitality and hierarchical notation is the problem of an array of coordinate classes which is longer than the notational base; for example, in the Public administration section of UDC there are listed twenty-five departments of central government, each of which is coordinate with the others; but the notational base is 0-9, so that we would expect the hierarchical notation to break down:

354	Ministries
354.1	Foreign Office
354.2	Colonial Office
354.3	Commonwealth Relations Office
etc, down to:	
354.24	Insurance
354.25	Food

Realising this, the compilers extended the base for coordinate classes by using two digits for all the subclasses of 354, so allowing up to 90 coordinate classes to have notation of the same length:

354	Ministries
354.11	Foreign Office
354.12	Colonial Office
354.13	Commonwealth Relations Office
etc, down to:	
354.86	Food

This is called 'group notation', or in UDC 'centesimal notation'.

In CC the same problem is met by the use of 'sector notation', in which the final digit of the series is reserved as a 'repeater'—on the principle that if this digit is ignored the notations will look coordinate (a doubtful principle—if a hierarchical notation requires a mental effort on the part of clients to recognise it, then it is not hierarchical):

9	Ventilation etc
91	Domestic water supply
92	House drainage
93	Ventilation
94	Heating
95	Lighting
98	Sanitary fitting
996	Lightning protection

One last problem of hospitality: we may need to specify proper names in our application of the classification scheme, for documents which deal with individual members of a class —for example, we may wish to keep all criticisms of *Hamlet* together, and all criticsms of *Macbeth*, within the class

WORKS ABOUT SHAKESPEARE'S PLAYS; or, within the class MOTORWAYS IN KENT, we may wish to differentiate works on the M25 from works on the M20 (especially as the building of the M25 is a matter of controversy). If we cannot do this, then our clients may need to search through all the works in a lengthy sequence with the same class mark, hoping to find those on the individual he is interested in. This happens in my college library, which has several shelves of books on classification schemes, but does not include the name of the scheme in the class mark; so that the works on any particular scheme are haphazardly scattered within the class by author's name. This is very irritating if I am about to lecture on, say, LC, and want to see the complete range of works as quickly as possible.

For this purpose we could simply add the name of the individual to the class notation. This is acceptable when that name is 'M25' or 'LC', but names such as 'Lady Mary Wortley Montagu' or 'The civilisation of the renaissance in Italy' are too long. A systematic method for abbreviating names for use with notation is provided by the Cutter-Sanborn table which enables the classifier to construct brief, unique codes which file in the same order as the full name; LC makes great use of these, and many are enumerated in the schedules of that scheme.

When we have to make a choice between conflicting properties of notation we should choose those which ensure unique codes with correct filing values, and ease of use; others—such as hierarchical notation and literal mnemonics— are inessential frills.

We may need to supplement the notation which represents classes from our scheme, by symbols which represent the sequence of documents in which the work in hand is to file (eg, the prefix R for a work to be placed in the reference section, or, BC's 7 as a prefix for works which are to go in a special collection), and by symbols which individualise the work, by specifying details such as author's name, copy number and date of publication. We might call the first kind of supplementary notation the 'collection number', and the second (which is far less generally used—the class notation, including form of presentation, and the collection number being sufficient for most libraries' needs) 'the document number'.

REFERENCES

1 Bliss, op cit.
2 Ranganathan, S R *Prolegomena* (op cit).

NINE

NOTATION: III

NOW THAT we are aware of the choices to be made when designing notation we can add a set to our own Zoology scheme. I have, in fact, provided three sets although, of course, only one is necessary; this is to illustrate more of the properties we have discussed. All three of the notations shown below are divisible and expressive. The first uses upper case letters and is retroactive and hierarchical; the second is an ordinal notation using numerals, with facet indicators in the form of arbitrary symbols; and the third is again hierarchical and based on upper case letters, but is expressive through the use of A as fence.

Zoology	A	1	B
(Form of presentation facet)			
Essays	BC	(1)	CC
Periodicals	BD	(2)	CD
(Operations facet)			
Collection	CD	:1	DC
Experiments	CE	:2	DD
Field experiments	CED	:3	DDC
Laboratory experiments	CEE	:4	DDD
Identification	CF	:5	DE
Classification/Taxonomy	CFD	:6	DEC
Naming/Nomenclature	CFE	:7	DED
(General processes facet)			
Development/Maturation	DE	=1	EC
Adaptation	DF	=2	ED
(Activities facet)			
Activities/Behaviour	EF	;1	FC
Social behaviour	EFF	;2	FCC
Play	EFFF	;3	FCCC
Hibernation	EFG	;4	FCD
Migration	EFH	;5	FCE
(Attributes facet)			
Intelligence	FG	'1'	GC
Aggression	FH	'2'	GD

(Physiological processes and parts facet)			
Anatomy	GH	,1	HC
(NB: particular parts are enumerated with their function or system below)			
Physiology	GJ	,2	HD
Skin	GJH	,22	HDC
Nervour system	GJJ	,3	HDD
Brain	GJJH	,31	HDDC
Senses	GJJJH	,4	HDDDC
Respiration/Breathing	GJK	,42	HDE
Locomotion	GJL	,5	HDF
Running	GJLH	,6	HDFC
Flying	GJLJ	,62	HDFD
Reproduction	GJM	,7	HDG
(Animals facet)			
Animals/Fauna	H	−11	J
(by effect on man subfacet)			
Beneficial animals	HJH	−12	JCC
Harmful animals	HJJ	−13	JCD
Venomous/Poisonous animals	HJJH	−14	JCDD
(by habit subfacet)			
Hibernating animals	HKJ	−21	JDC
Migratory animals	HKK	−22	JDD
(by habitat subfacet)			
(by land form subfacet)			
Coastal animals	HLJ	−31	JEC
Littoral/Sea shore animals	HLJJ	−32	JECC
Lowland animals	HLK	−33	JED
Upland animals	HLL	−34	JEE
Hill animals	HLLJ	−35	JEEC
Mountain animals	HLLK	−36	JEED
(by ground cover facet)			
Desert animals	HMJ	−41	JFC
Grassland animals	HMK	−42	JFD
Scrubland animals	HML	−43	JFE
Woodland/Forest animals	HMM	−44	JFF
Jungle animals	HMMJ	−45	JFFC
(by latitude subfacet)			
Polar animals	HNJ	−51	JGC
Temperate zone animals	HNK	−52	JGD
Tropical animals	HNL	−53	JGE
Equatorial animals	HNLJ	−54	JGEC
(by element subfacet)			
Aquatic/Water animals	HOJ	−61	JHC
Fresh water animals	HOJJ	−62	JHCC
River animals	HOJJJ	−63	JHCCC
Lake animals	HOJJK	−64	JHCCD
Marine/Sea/Salt water animals	HOJK	−65	JHCD

96

Amphibious animals	HOK	−66	JHD

(notations from the subclasses of WATER ANIMALS may be added to this notation as appropriate; for brevity the first three letters of the added notations from the alphabetical sets may be omitted—eg the notations for the class AMPHIBIOUS LAKE ANIMALS would be HOKHK and JHDCD)

Land animals	HOL	−67	JHE
(by zoologists' taxonomy subfacet)			
Invertebrates	HP	−69	JJ
Arachnids	HPJ	−71	JJC
Spiders	HPJJ	−711	JJCC
Insects	HPK	−72	JJD
Lepidoptera	HPKJ	−73	JJDC
Moths	HPKJJ	−74	JJDCC
Leaf Moths	HPKJJJ	−75	JJDCCC
Butterflies	HPKJK	−751	JJDCD
Hymenoptera	HPKK	−76	JJDD
Bees	HPKKJ	−77	JJDDC
Honeybees	HPKKJJ	−78	JJDDCC
Vertebrates	HQ	−79	JK
Fish	HQJ	−791	JKC
Amphibians	HQK	−81	JKD
Frogs	HQKJ	−811	JKDC
Toads	HQKK	−82	JKDD
Reptiles	HQL	−821	JKE
Lizards	HQLJ	−822	JKEC
Snakes	HQLK	−833	JKED
Tortoises	HQLL	−834	JKEE
Birds	HQM	−84	JKF
Raptors/Birds of prey	HQMJ	−85	JKFC
Eagles	HQMJJ	−86	JKFCC
Golden eagles	HQMJJJ	−87	JKFCCC
Mammals	HQN	−88	JKG
Rodents	HQNJ	−89	JKGC
Rats	HQNJJ	−90	JKGCC
Procyonidae	HQNK	−91	JKGD
Pandas	HQNKJ	−92	JKGDC
Bears	HQNL	−93	JKGE
Pandas	HQNLJ	−94	JKGEC
Primates	HQNM	−95	JKGF
Monkeys	HQNMJ	−96	JKGFC
Colobus monkeys	HQNMJJ	−97	JKGFCC
Man	HQNMK	−99	JKGFD

Notation for phase relationships

At this stage we can give a notation to all the works on which our scheme was based except two—documents 12 and 39. These works are on complex classes, and as yet we have no symbols to represent phase relationships. These symbols are needed so that the relationships may be precisely expressed, and so that the resulting notation files correctly— before any subdivisions of the phase which is cited first, and before any synthesised notation for superimposed or compound classes. The symbols need to maintain expressiveness.

In CC, Ranganathan recognises five phase relationships— general, difference, comparison, influence and bias—and allows three symbols for each relationship, to be used according to whether the phases are from different facets, from within the same facet or from within the same array. The symbols are lower-case letters, and they are introduced by &. For example, 'comparison' in the class COMPARISON BETWEEN PAINTING AND SCULPTURE is represented by &c, giving the notation ND&cNQ (in which ND means Sculpture and NQ Painting); but in the class COMPARISON BETWEEN WATER COLOUR AND OIL PAINTING it is shown by &v, in NQ,3&vNQ,4 (where NQ,3 means Water colour and NQ,4 Oil painting). In the first example the phases are different canonical classes and are, therefore, necessarily from different facets; while in the second case the phases are obviously from the same array. The provision of fifteen different symbols seems unnecessarily precise; perhaps we could content ourselves with one for each different relationship, as does BC2. Let us also limit ourselves to two relationships, omitting bias (which we have suggested is best regarded as a form of presentation), difference (which seems a little too like comparison) and general (which hardly seems worth specifying). As we have not used lower-case letters in the three notations it is convenient to use these as phase relators; say, a to represent comparison and b to represent influence.

Before we can apply these we must choose the citation orders between the phases of complex classes. In a comparison phase relationship no direction is involved (that is, PAINTING COMPARED WITH SCULPTURE is the same as

98

SCULPTURE COMPARED WITH PAINTING); in this case, there is no basis for a choice of citation order, and it is usual to cite first the phase which files first. The same is true of the general and the difference relationships. The influence phase, on the other hand, is directional: THE INFLUENCE OF PAINTING ON SCULPTURE is not the same as THE INFLUENCE OF SCULPTURE ON PAINTING. Here, we should want to keep documents on the phase which is influenced together, giving the citation order Influenced phase—Influencing phase. Bias phase, if we were including it, is similarly directional: STATISTICS FOR NURSES is not the same as NURSING FOR STATISTICIANS. In this case we should keep the work with its subject, not with the discipline for whose practitioners it is written—*Statistics for nurses* is about statistics, not nursing.

Now we can classify all the works in our list. The result for ten of them is shown overleaf. As the citation order for the two alphabetical notations is not easily changed, I have chosen a different one for the notation with facet indicators: Physiology—Attributes—Activities—General processes—Animals—Operations—Form.

2)	Essays on the physiology of marine fauna	HOJKGJBC	1,2−65(1)	JHCDAHDACC
4)	Laboratory experiments in the respiration of vertebrates	HQGJKCEE	1,42−79:4	JKAGJKADDD
12)	The role of play in the development of primates	HQNMDEbHQNMEFF	1−9561;3−95	JKGFAECbJKGFAFCCC
14)	The insect integument	HPKGJH	1,22−72	JJDAHDC
24)	Salt water fish	HQJHOJK	1−791−65	JKCAJHCD
31)	Entomological taxonomy (a periodical)	HPKCFDBD	1:6−72(2)	JJDADECACD
32)	Hibernation	EFG	1;4	FCD
34)	The intelligence of rats	HQNJJFG	1'1'−90	JKGCCAGC
39)	A comparison between frogs and toads	HQKJaHQKK	1−811a1)82	JKDCaJKDD
40)	Mammalian reproduction	HQNGJM	1,7−88	JKGAHDG

TEN

THE ALPHABETICAL SUBJECT INDEX

AN INDEX, in the narrow sense used in this chapter, is a
list of terms in a known order, which shows their location in
some other sequence whose order is not obvious. We need to
provide this sort of index for our scheme, to save the time of
the cataloguer or indexer using it. All we have to do is to re-
arrange the terms which represent the classes in the scheme
into alphabetical order, and show the notation for the class
which each term represents:

Activities	EF
Adaptation	DF
Aggression	FH
Amphibians	HQK
Amphibious animals	HOK
Anatomy	GH
Animals	H

and so on down to

Tortoises	HQLL
Tropical animals	HNL
Upland animals	HLL
Venomous animals	HJJH
Vertebrates	HQ
Woodland animals	HMM
Zoology	A

Of course we shall include each synonym in its proper place
in the sequence: under F we shall place

Fauna	H

and under P

Poisonous animals   HJJH

whose synonyms have already been given in the excerpt above (There is no point in referring from one synonym to another—Fauna *see* Animals takes more time to write or type than Fauna H ; and, more important, it makes the cataloguer's life less easy). In addition, we may have to distinguish homographs, so that the cataloguer knows which of the notations is relevant to the work he is dealing with. This is best done by adding a qualifying term which represents a superordinate class:

| Pandas: Bears | HQNLJ |
| Pandas: Procyonidae | HQNKJ |

This sort of index, in which each entry term has one notation, is sometimes called a 'specific index'.(1) The synonym, 'one-place index', is perhaps a better name—especially as the type of index to which the one-place index is usually contrasted is equally specific. The one-place index is efficient when each concept appears at one place in the schedules only, as in our simple faceted scheme; but when the same concept appears in different contexts, as will happen with an enumerative scheme or with a larger-scale faceted scheme, then more than one notation must be shown against the terms which represent such concepts. For a scheme of this kind we must construct a 'relative index'.(2)

Dewey said that his relative index (another of his inventions) was the most important part of DC (3). The name is derived from the fact that this sort of index displays relationships, by bringing together under the name of a concept all the notations under which it is scattered in the schedules—here is an example based on DC:

Children: Care	649.1
Children: Medicine	618.92
Children: Psychology	155.4
Children: Social welfare	362.7

A relative index is constructed by the method we used above to distinguish the two meanings of the term 'pandas'; that is, sufficient terms representing superordinate classes are added after the entry term to make the context in which a particular notation is appropriate clear. The technique is called 'chain indexing'(4), because it is based on the analysis of the chain of subordinate classes. For example, the class READING IN PRIMARY SCHOOLS would, in DC, produce this chain:

Education   (370)
  Schools   (371)
    Primary   (372)
      Curriculum   (372.19)
        Reading   (372.4)

which would yield the following index entries:

Reading: Primary schools   372.4
Curriculum: Primary schools   372.19
Subjects: Primary schools   372.19 ('Subjects' is a synonym for 'curriculum')
Primary schools   372
Elementary schools   372 ('Elementary schools' = 'Primary schools')
Schools   371
Education   370

Notice that entries such as Primary schools: Reading 372.4 are not made; if we were to include these we should merely be repeating the display of relationships already made in the schedules.

Relative indexes are easy to construct, but some schemes do have bad indexes. As usual, DC provides an example (the index to DC17 had to be replaced free of charge to all purchasers, because of its inefficiencies). Not only does DC18 make 'see' references between synonyms, but it does so with lack of care which is peculiarly irritating. As it happens, on the day I typed the final draft of this section I had given a class an exercise on DC; one of the works to be classified was called *The law of children*. Students looked in the index under 'Children'; found, to begin with, that entries are made under 'Child', 'Children' and 'Children's' apparently indiscriminately, so that all three sequences had to be checked; discovered that 'Law' was not present as a qualifier in any of then; found a reference 'other aspects see Young people'; checked there, and found, sure enough, 'Young people:— Law'—but as another reference, leading to 'Minors: Law'! Further, DC18 uses different synonyms for different purposes—'Horse' is used in the context of riding or racing or cookery, but 'Equidae' for the zoological aspects of the animal; refers from narrower classes which have no specific notation to broader classes (eg 'Persian cats see Long-haired cats') instead of merely giving the notation for the broader class at the entry for the narrower; and contains errors (such as indexing Social welfare to the notation 360, which is in fact the portmanteau class Social pathology, social services and association; and indexing Law libraries as 026.43, when it should be 026.34). The result is an index which is suspect, and difficult to use.

REFERENCES

1 Sayers's term; see his *Manual of classification for librarians* 5th ed, by Arthur Maltby, London, Deutsch, 1975.

2 Ibid.

3 Introduction to DC 12, reprinted in successive editions including the current DC18.

4 Mills, J 'Chain indexing and the classified catalogue' *Library Association record* April 1955 (and see succeeding issues for correspondence).

ELEVEN

GENERAL CLASSIFICATION SCHEMES

SO FAR we have discussed the creation of a classification scheme for a limited area of knowledge only—a special scheme, taking for our example the subject Zoology. We might suppose that when we have to cater for a collection of documents covering the whole of knowledge, we would merely need to apply a collection of special schemes which between them contained all the necessary classes: but this is not so. To avoid wasteful repetition and ambiguities a unified general collection of documents needs a unified general classification scheme, which reflects a single view of the structure of knowledge. Such schemes have their uses for compilers of special schemes too. They provide context for the special scheme (for example, when we delimited the subject area of our special scheme we must have done so with an awareness of its containing class Biology and the yet broader class Science); they provide for the fringe subjects which any special scheme needs (the scientific techniques in our Operations facet are not peculiar to Zoology, and could have been derived from a general scheme; again, the compiler of a scheme on Librarianship need not list all types of libraries by subject—Medical libraries, Heraldry libraries, Chemistry libraries etc—when there is a general scheme to draw on); and they provide common facets to further reduce the work of the compiler of a special scheme.

This is probably the place to point out that the existence of general schemes does not make the compilation of special schemes unnecessary. It is not enough to lift out appropriate sections from a general scheme for use in a special library, first because general schemes are usually not detailed enough for specialist collections; second, because the unified view of the structure of knowledge reflected in the general scheme may not suit the needs of the special scheme (for example, most general schemes would probably place works on Zoo buildings in Architecture—along with Museum buildings, Art galleries and so on—while in our Zoology scheme we could place them in the Habitats facet); third, because to take sections from a general scheme wastes notation (if we had simply used DC's Zoology class for our scheme we should have been restricted to the notation 590 and its subdivisions); and last, because most general schemes are anyway not very efficient.(1)

The structure of general schemes
The basis for the overall structure of all current general scheme is the main class. Main classes are conventional divisions of the universe of knowledge, which may in general be regarded as coordinate classes which together exhaust the universe, and within which the techniques of enumeration and facet analysis we have discussed in this book are applied (these statements are not true of CC, which contains some classes, called 'partially comprehensive classes', which are superordinate to other main classes; and whose main classes sometimes have subclasses, called 'canonical classes', within which facet analysis takes place rather than in the main class itself(2)).

Again, all modern schemes are aspect, or disciplinary, schemes; that is, their main classes reflect the specialisations apparent in society, as in DC, whose main classes include Religion, Science, Technology, and Art; CC, which has main classes such as Physics, Biology, Art and Religion; and BC, with Astronomy, Education, Religion, Economics, Technology, Art and so on. The term 'aspect schemes' refers to the quality of collocating aspects of entities which such schemes possess; for example, in DC works on the things called Firearms may be found in class 739.74 when they deal with firearms as art objects (collocated with works on ornamental ironwork, fine watches, artistic jewellery and precious metalwork); in 623.4 when they deal with the engineering aspects of firearms (along with works on the engineering aspects of protection against nuclear attack, on guided

106

missiles, and on military aircraft engineering); in 355.82, when they deal with firearms from the military administrator's point of view (together with works on food, clothing, transport and communication equipment and medical supplies treated from the same point of view); and possibly in 399, when they deal with the customs associated with weapons (along with other war customs and ceremonies, such as war dances, peace pipes and scalping). Of course, in collocating aspects, disciplinary schemes scatter works on entities, as the Firearms example shows—the client looking for all information on Firearms could find DC a frustrating scheme to use. On the other hand, specialists (museum officials and collectors, engineers, staff officers and military tacticians and strategists, and sociologists and anthropologists) would find collocation by specialisation very helpful; and it seems probable that, in a general library, this approach by discipline is more common—that more clients are likely to want to find all documents on military science together than are likely to want to find everything on firearms together, for example.

Even the client interested in the entity rather than the aspect may not find the scattering by aspect too irritating, because the works found in different locations will be quite different in content (a work on firearms as collectable objects does not contain the same information as a work on the use of firearms in war), and the scattering could help him to structure his research. I remember a social welfare student at Stevenage College, where I was tutor-librarian, having to write an extended essay on the family. When he came to the library for help he was at first annoyed to find that not all books on this topic were together on the shelves (because DC, the scheme we were using, scatters works on the entity Family according to aspects such as Psychology, Sociology and Welfare), but then realised that this structure—revealed on the shelves and in the catalogue—gave him the structure of his essay, and a plan to work to.

Disciplinary main classes produce a generally helpful grouping of documents, but they also produce problems for the indexer and the client. The obvious one is what is to be done with the work which deals with an entity in all its aspects— the book on firearms which covers their engineering, decoration, customs, uses, preservation and collection, for example. Three solutions are available to the compiler of an aspect scheme, or the indexer using one (another is to abandon disciplinary main classes; this is discussed below). The first solution is to place such a general work in the first disciplinary class of the scheme which contains the entity (for example, in UDC—which uses this solution—the general work on firearms would be placed in Military science); the second is to place the work in its 'uniquely defining class'(3) —that is, in that discipline which provides the only necessary definition of the entity (eg, for the entity Horse the uniquely defining class would be Zoology—not Military science, although horses are used in war; not Recreation, although horses are used for recreation; not Transport, nor Farming, nor Catering, although all of these classes could take works on aspects of the horse); the third is to reserve a class at the beginning of the scheme for such general works (BC2 is the only scheme to do this; the class is labelled 'Phenomena').

A more serious problem is that disciplinary main classes have what Bernard Palmer calls 'a very fixing effect'(4) on the structure of knowledge found in general classification schemes, while knowledge itself is not fixed. While the boundaries of knowledge are constantly enlarged, the relationships between different areas of knowledge changed, and the relative importance of different disciplines altered, aspects schemes tend to remain unaltered because of the strait-jacket restraint imposed by their main class structure. It is difficult to deal with inter-disciplinary subjects (so common today) in a scheme based on disciplines; difficult to change the allocation of notation to reflect the increase in importance or the decay of different disciplines; and difficult to insert entirely new disciplines within a disciplinary structure (a striking example is that the DC class 629— labelled 'Other branches of engineering'— is used to accommodate not only aircraft engineering, motor vehicle engineering and astronautics, but also automatic control engineering).

It is true that these difficulties are in essence notational only, and that they could be dealt with by revisions in new editions; but in practice revisions to the basic structure of general schemes are rarely made—partly because of the trouble they cause compilers, and partly because the re-classification of libraries which revisions imply make them unpopular with librarians (and clients). Incidentally, the unwillingness to change is shown clearly in the 629 example above: the order of the classes is as shown—that is, the class Astronautics is separated from its related class Aircraft engineering by Motor vehicle engineering. If compilers of schemes are unwilling to make the small change necessary to collocate Astronautics with Aircraft engineering, it is not likely that they will be eager to make more drastic changes in structure.

Alternatives to disciplinary main classes
This last problem could be re-stated in these terms: disciplinary main classes lack an absolute basis which would keep them valid whatever changes occur in the structure of knowledge. That disciplinary main classes are not absolute is easily shown, in that some schemes have ten main classes (eg DC, UDC), while others (eg LC and BC) have over twenty; that in CC, Agriculture is a main class, while in DC it is part of the main class Technology; that in BC, Social welfare is a main class, while in both DC and LC it is part of Social sciences; and so on. If we want an absolute, universally valid, basis for a general scheme we have to abandon such main classes, or abandon the use of main classes altogether.

The first alternative to traditional main classes, then, is to collocate by entity rather than by aspect; for example, we could keep all works on firearms together, while scattering works on collecting, military science, customs and engineering. Schemes which do this are called 'concrete' schemes, following the terminology of J D Brown, whose SC is an example. Brown refers to entities as concretes, and says 'the . . . concrete subject should be preferred to the more general standpoint'(5). His reason for this preference is that clients looking for information on an aspect—a 'more general standpoint'—are not always in search of a particular entity. For example, somebody looking for works on collecting may not be interested in firearms. On the other hand, when looking for information on a concrete a client will not be interested in works on other concretes. For example, when looking for works on firearms, a client will not want to see works on clocks and watches, or on ballistic missiles, or on military food supplies. Brown concludes, therefore, that interest in concretes is constant, but interest in aspects is occasional(6). This is a persuasive argument, but it ignores the point that collocation by discipline is more generally acceptable; and also the fact that, if we base our structure on disciplinary main classes, we are giving some help to the enquirer searching for information on an entity (as we argued above), and the reverse is not true—that is, if we collocate concretes we do not offer a useful alternative to the client who makes an approach by discipline.

The second possibility is to apply the technique of facet analysis to the universe of knowledge(7), rather than within 'postulated'(8) main classes; that is, we could abandon main classes as the basis of our scheme, which would consist of a series of comprehensive facets—an Operations facet, containing all materials, and so on. The general classification scheme on which the Classification Research Group worked (9) was originally to be based on conventional main classes, but this was later abandoned in favour of a structure of two facets, Entities and Attributes (Attributes including both Properties and Processes). Now, this certainly makes it easier to deal with the problems which disciplinary main classes produce for compilers and revisers of the scheme; but there are three objections to it. The first is that its use requires the application of the same citation order for all subjects, and it seems unlikely that the one chosen will be appropriate to them all. The second is that it would produce longer notations than does the conventional method of enumerating the same concept in different main classes(10). The third objection is that it merely moves the problems back a stage, and does not eliminate them. Imagine a general scheme composed of the two facets Entities and Attributes. If we choose the citation order Entities—Attributes we produce an order of documents very similar to that which results from the application of a concrete scheme; if we choose the other order, the result would be much the same as that produced

110

by the use of an aspect scheme. As Palmer says:

'Have the group (ie CRG), perhaps, in their efforts to avoid the premature construction of main classes during the present state of flux, only succeeded in re-introducing them by the back door, so to speak?'(11)

Order of main classes

If we agree with Derek Austin (who, by the way, worked on the CRG scheme) when he says:

'While it may be easy to question on theoretical grounds the extent to which knowledge can be broken down into watertight compartments, from the practical viewpoint of library organization main classes confer such obvious advantages that if they had not evolved already we should have to invent them'(12)

we have to accept an overall structure based on main classes; and we have to place them in an order. It is commonly, and rightly, argued that this order does not affect the efficiency of a classification scheme to any great extent, because clients are only concerned with order and collocation within the main class they are interested in—for example, the client looking for books on the tuning of car engines needs a helpful order within the class Technology, but is not at all affected by the order between this and other classes—his search is neither helped nor hindered if the previous class is Agriculture (as it is in LC) rather than Science (as it is in DC). According to Ranganathan, 'the order of the main classes in the layout of a scheme of classification is not of much moment as long as it is reasonably tolerable.'(13)

Two principles will help us to produce a 'tolerable' main class order: related main classes should be collocated, and main classes which depend on others, or which developed from, or later than, others, should follow them. Observance of the first principle is seen whenever classes which tend to be studied together are kept together (one of the criticisms of DC's order and collocation of main classes is its separation of Language and Literature, which in other schemes—even UDC—are collocated); whenever classes which may be considered to be part of a greater whole are kept together (as in the collocation of Social sciences, Politics, Law and

111

Education in LC); and whenever applications are kept with the sciences on which they are based (as when BC collocates Chemical technology with Chemistry, and CC keeps Agriculture with Botany). There may, though, be conflict between these three expressions of the principle; for example, literature is an art and should be collocated with other arts as part of a greater whole—but is language, which is studied along with literature, part of that same greater whole? A good example of this clash is provided by CC, which includes this among its sequence of main classes:

I Botany
J Agriculture
K Zoology
KZ Animal husbandry

This is an example of application-with-science, but it obviously separates two main classes normally studied together (Agriculture and Animal husbandry) and two main classes which form a greater whole (Zoology and Botany, which are the two branches of Biology). Keeping applications with their sciences also causes unhelpful collocation when practised with mindless consistency—I was shocked by SC long before I became a librarian, because it keeps works on fencing and on archery with Military science (from which they were, of course, derived) rather than with other sports. As is so often the case in classification, we cannot satisfy everyone by our decisions—but at least we should be aware of all the possibilities (and the needs of our clients) before we make them.

The second principle is really a set of two: that the order between main classes should follow the order of their evolution, or should reflect the dependence of one on another. A good example of the first is provided by SC, whose main classes reflect, according to its compiler, the evolutionary sequence Matter+Force—Life—Mind—Record (eg Physical sciences—Biology—Philosophy—Literature). The most striking example of dependence is Bliss's order for his BC, based on what he calls gradation in speciality—the principle that a discipline whose study depends on techniques or ideas from some other discipline should follow that discipline. For

112

example, astronomers use techniques and tools from Chemistry and Physics—optics, spectroscopy etc—so that Astronomy should file after these two classes; chemists use techniques from Physics, so Chemistry should follow Physics; physicists make use of Mathematics, so the filing order of these two classes should be Mathematics—Physics. This idea, with help from others presented in this section, produces in BC the most satisfying order of main classes of any of the current schemes (here shown in a slightly simplified form):

Philosophy
  Mathematics
    Physics
      Chemistry
        Astronomy
          Earth sciences
            Biology
              Botany
              Zoology
              Man
                  Medicine
                  Psychology

                  Education
                  Social sciences
                    History
                    Religion
                    Social welfare
                    Politics
                    Public administration
                    Law
                    Economics

                  Technology

                  Arts

                  Language and literature

As we have seen, the CRG scheme avoided the problems of arbitrary and rigid main classes by applying facet analysis to the whole of knowledge. It still required an overall order, corresponding to main class order in a conventional scheme:

an order of entities. D J Foskett(15) advocated the use of the theory of integrative levels, first advanced by a bio-chemist, Joseph Needham. Integrative levels is an evolution-ary idea, which produces an absolute order of entities based on their increasing complexity, which results from the addition of qualities. At certain stages in the progession from simple to complex, the additional qualities result in a new level of organisation; for example, a vertebrate is more than just an invertebrate with the addition of a backbone. Con-sider this sequence:

Cells
Tissues
Organs
Systems
Organisms

Each of these entities is composed of its predecessors: organisms (such as sharks and earwigs) are made up of systems (the digestive system, the nervous system etc); systems are composed of organs (mouth, gullet, stomach. . .); organs are made of tissue; and cells are the components of tissue. But these entities are not mere aggregations of their predecessors; each successive entity displays a more complex organisation than its predecessor—for example, a system is a set of organs which interact in the performance of a function, and an organism is a set of systems which cooperate in the maintenance of the organism. The result is that organisms all have qualities (eg independent life) not shared by systems; systems have qualities not shared by organs; and so on. It is this principle of levels of organisation which determines the order of entities, and which articulates their sequence in the classification scheme. Here is part of one of the outline sequences which CRG researchers produced:

(Physical level)
1   fundamental particles
11   atoms
111   molecules
1V   molecular assemblages

(Chemical level)
1   elements
11   compounds
111 complex compounds
(Non-living masses)
1   minerals
11   rocks
111 physiographic features
1V astronomical entities
(Biological level)
1   viruses
11   organelles
111 cells
1V tissues
etc

As we have seen, Palmer believes that this theory merely moves the problems associated with main classes back, to be dealt with by the indexer rather than by the compiler of the scheme. Still, it provides a good basis for order between things; whether this would produce a *better* overall structure for a general scheme seems doubtful. One of the points made in its favour is that the resulting overall order is rather similar to that found in BC, which is generally agreed to be very helpful (Mills mentions this in his introductions to the different volumes of BC2). This is true; but it is worth saying that Bliss's order is based on his perception of a relationship between documents, while the order of integrative levels is an absolute order which does not reflect such relationships. Perhaps we should do better to use an order which suits human perceptions (even though this may have to be revised as the perceptions change) rather than a more 'scientific' order, which does not.

Common facets
In the second edition of DC, 1885, Dewey incorporated a list of documentary forms whose notations could be synthesised with any subject notation; this avoided the wasteful enumeration of such forms—dictionaries, periodicals etc—under every subject. This is an example of a common facet, the

other usual ones being facets of time and place (although a number of others are available in different schemes). In DC these common facets are now called 'standard subdivisions'; in UDC 'common auxiliaries'; and in BC 'systematic schedules'. This principle may be extended to concepts which may be applicable only to certain classes in the scheme; for example, in the Zoology class of DC, animal activities such as respiration are listed once only:

591.1 Physiology of animals
591.14 Secretion and excretion
591.15 Genetics
591.16 Reproduction
etc,

leaving the expression of compounds of these activities and particular organisms to synthesis. For example, the class ELEPHANTS is enumerated with the notation 599.61; the class REPRODUCTION IN ELEPHANTS is expressed by synthesis—599.610416 (in which 04 acts as a facet indicator). BC1 had 'special systematic schedules' and UDC has 'special auxiliaries' to serve the same purpose. We need to provide common facets in any modern general scheme.

Form classes
In a general classification scheme, some main classes are not susceptible to arrangement by subject. One of these is the Generalia class, which takes works of such generality that they cannot fit into any main class. Because there is no way in which we can distinguish one document from another by their subject in such a class—they all cover everything—we have to use the physical form of the document (eg periodical) or its form of presentation (eg encyclopaedia) as the basis for arrangement. The GENERALIA class is therefore called a form class. (It is worth noting, though, that most Generalia classes do include some subject divisions—eg DC's includes LIBRARIANSHIP and JOURNALISM. SC's included what Brown called 'pervasive subjects'(17)—those which are universally useful, such as MATHEMATICS, or those which make use of all subjects, such as EDUCATION).

The other obvious form class is LITERATURE. Literary works may be arranged by their subject (after all, *Fiction*

116

index is a subject index to novels and short stories), but it is more useful to collocate by language and by form, so that all German works are together, and within that all German novels. We would not want to keep *Troilus and Criseyde* with *Troilus and Cressida*, although they are obviously on the same subject; we would rather keep Chaucer's poem with other English poetry, and Shakespeare's play with other English plays. This reflects the way in which literary works are used: having read *Caprice* we are less likely to say to the librarian 'Have you got any more novels about stage-struck young girls?' than 'Have you got any more novels by Ronald Firbank?' (assuming, that is, that anyone having finished one Firbank novel would want to read another immediately!) Of course the Literature class will include some works which must be arranged by subject—those which are *about* literature; it is only for *examples* of literature that it is a form class.

REFERENCES
1 Sayer's Manual (op cit.)
2 for partially comprehensive classes see Ranganathan, S R *Colon classification* 6th ed, Bombay; London, Asia Publishing House, 1960 (chapter 1—Main classes) for canonical classes see his *Library classification—fundamentals and procedure* Madras, Madras Library Association; London, Goldston, 1944.
3 Farradane, J (et al) *Information retrieval by relational indexing*; part 1, methodology. London, City University, 1966.
4 Palmer, Bernard *Itself an education* Library Association, 1962.
5 Brown, James Duff *Subject classification* 3rd ed, by James D Stewart Grafton, 1939.
6 Ibid.
7 Foskett D J *Classification for a general index language* Library Association, 1970.
8 for the status of postulates see Ranganathan, S R *Prolegomena*, (op cit) page 396.
9 Foskett, D J *Classification for a general index language* (op cit).

10) Austin, Derek 'Trends towards a compatible general system' Maltby, Arthur *Classification in the 1970's* Bingley, 1972.

11) Palmer, op cit.

12) Austin, op cit.

13) Ranganathan, S R *Prolegomena to library classification* lst ed, Bombay; London, Asia Publishing House, 1937. Ranganathan, S R General and special classifications *Classification research: proceedings of the Second International Study Conference*, 1964. Copenhagen, Munksgaard, 1965.

14) Bliss, op cit.

15) Foskett, D J 'Classification and integrative levels' Foskett D J and Palmer, B I *Sayer's memorial volume* Library Association, 1961.

16) Mills, J *Modern outline* (op cit).

17) Brown, op cit.

TWELVE

OBJECTIONS TO SYSTEMATIC ORDER

OF COURSE we have assumed in this book that systematic order achieved through the use of a classification scheme is helpful; but we ought to consider its limitations and the objections to it.

Systematic order between documents is not entirely successful because documents have many different relationships, and systematic order can only display one. This has already been exemplified in our examination of citation order; when we choose a citation order we decide which subjects are to have their documents collocated—and, therefore, which are to have theirs scattered. Classification applied to shelf order scatters more related documents than it collocates. Again, we may have to use attributes of documents other than their subjects as the basis for shelf order—for example, most libraries have parallel sequences of documents based on their size (ordinary sized books, oversize books); their physical form (it is not a good idea to keep gramophone records with music scores, for example, because the records are likely to be damaged; therefore the related works are scattered); or conditions of use (reference works, lending works, works to which access is restricted). We would claim that these separations can be corrected by the use of the catalogue (with multiple entries and references), and their effect mitigated by good guiding and personal service from the librarian; but we cannot deny that the good effect of systematic order between documents has been vitiated.

Even within a particular sequence, and in a section unaffected by citation order scattering, related documents may not be collocated; and, unrelated documents may be brought together. In her investigations into the efficiency of classification, Dr Kelley[1] discovered that a very small percentage of material on a subject available in a library was found at the notation for that subject—for example, only 2.22% for the subject BUFFALOES. The other material was found under superordinate classes—BOVINE ANIMALS, RUMINANTS, HOOFED ANIMALS, MAMMALS, VERTEBRATES —whose books give some information on buffaloes (more information was also found in parts of the library not related to zoology, such as American history). Now, these broader classes were separated from the class BUFFALOES by many classes which did not contain information on this subject—for example, between MAMMALS and BUFFALOES the client if likely to find works on kangaroos, elephants, horses, rhinoceroses and so on. Dr Kelley concluded from this that systematic order is unhelpful beyond a certain level of specificity, and suggested the use of broad classification for shelf order. We can see that this is not very helpful—it merely substitutes haphazard scattering by author's name within a broad class for the systematic, and therefore intelligible, scattering of specific classification; and it ignores the importance of what Mills calls 'a valuable instrument in assisting readers'[2]—the display of broader-narrower relationships on the shelves.

The second problem, that systematic order brings unrelated material together, is a theoretical difficulty only. It is true that there are abrupt breaks within sequences when classes are succeeded by others in a new area of knowledge; for example, when one class is the last in a main class and the next is the first in the succeeding main class, as in this sequence from DC:

797 (Water & air sports)—798 (Equestrian sports)—
799 (Hunting)—800 (Literature)

but this has no practical bad effects.

Another objection to classification is that its practitioners have tended to ignore certain relationships. In some areas of knowledge, or for some particular documents, concepts such as the methodology used or the approach of the author may be more important for some clients than the subjects of

120

works; and although these may be expressed in some classification schemes they are often forgotten—and even when used, they are subordinated to subject. It is for this sort of reason that Professor Swift and his colleagues(3) feel that traditional classification techniques are actively unhelpful in some fields of the social sciences; and their views echo those of Dr Kelley forty years ago, who thought that classifiers should more often be concerned with the intended use or purpose of documents than with their subjects. Even within the area of subject classification, traditional classification tends to ignore what Karen Sparck Jones calls 'semantically non-obvious relationships'(4), concentrating on the display of generic relationships based on the meanings of concepts, and so making it more difficult for clients to make other links which could be fruitful. This is one of the advantages which keyword classification has, according to Sparck Jones—its relationships are statistically derived rather than semantically derived, and they are not the obvious ones.

These objections come together in one great accusation against classification used to produce systematic order: that it establishes one structure of knowledge in the minds of all users of libraries. This blinkers students, thinkers, research workers, and tends to make them follow traditional paths. We can argue that any structure applied to collections of documents would have that effect; that any structure allows its users to seek relationships other than those it displays (indeed, that the display of obvious relationships frees clients to seek non-obvious ones, through lateral thinking); and that, in any case, alternative structures can be displayed in catalogues and indexes. But we cannot escape the fact that library classification is a very powerful tool, and that among its side-effects may be the conditioning of its users to accept as absolute the structure it displays—and we should strive to lessen this effect.

There is one answer to all objections to the use of systematic order: that so far no better way of arranging documents has been devised; and, as we have said, it is a useful base for other indexing tools and techniques. We may not go as far as Langridge, who said 'there is no substitute for classification'(5), but we can agree with Maltby:

'The real issue confronting ... critics is to find a constructive and viable alternative to classification that can serve most library situations so well—for, despite the difficulties, classification *is* a good servant.'(6)

REFERENCES

1 Kelley, Grace O *The classification of books—an inquiry into its usefulness to the reader* New York, Wilson, 1937.

2 Mills, J *Modern outline* (op cit).

3 Watson, L E (et al) 'Sociology and information science' *Journal of librarianship*, v. 5, no 4, October 1973.

4 Jones, Karen Sparck *Automatic keyword classification* Butterworths, 1971.

5 Langridge, op cit.

6 Maltby, Arthur 'Classification—logic, limits, levels' *Drexel library quarterly* 10 (4) October 1974.

THIRTEEN

AUTOMATIC CLASSIFICATION

WHEN I mentioned to a colleague that I was to write this book, he commented that it would probably be an obituary work; he meant by this that classification by human intellectual effort will shortly be superseded by computerised indexing techniques. This has been the hope of all advocates of mechanised systems of indexing since Mortimer Taube, who thought that his Uniterm system would solve all indexing problems without benefit of classification.(1) (It did not, of course—most post-coordinate systems like Uniterm now use controlled, structured index vocabularies called thesauri, which are classificatory tools—indeed, many modern thesauri are based on faceted schemes, and are sometimes published with them, as in Jean Aitchison's *Thesaurofacet*(2).) This hope stems partly from antagonism to classification, either rational or emotional; partly from a desire to use new tools, and to justify this by denigrating old ones; and partly from a genuine belief that mechanised techniques produce, or could produce, better indexing systems. As Richmond says:

'Some of the more interesting adventures in information science ... stemmed from an irremedial loss of faith in classification as a way of organising knowledge.'(3)

Such 'adventures' have sometimes resulted in systems which have toppled classification from its traditional place; perhaps the most striking of these is the replacement of the classified catalogue by a computer-produced KWOC (Key-Word Out of Context) catalogue at Bath University(4). However, reports of the death of classification are premature —or, as Mark Twain said of newspaper reports of his own death, greatly exaggerated. While the need for systematic order of documents remains, or while we still need controlled

123

and structured index languages to increase precision and recall, classification will still be necessary—and, for the moment, this means human classification. Still, attempts have been made to group documents and document surrogates, and index terms, without human intellectual effort; that is, to imitate the good effects of human classification by the use of the computer. We shall examine some of these in this chapter.

As has often been said, the computer is not intelligent—it is an 'idiot'(5); or, rather, it is no more than a machine. It is not able to understand the meaning of terms, nor to appreciate the relationships between them. We might assume from this that even an approximation to concept indexing cannot be achieved through the use of the computer alone. Still, this machine can count, and it can compare or match items of information; and these are powerful facilities which have been used to produce groupings of things automatically.

Document clustering
Document surrogates may be grouped using the computer's counting and matching operations; this is illustrated in Salton's SMART system, which he and his associates worked on at Cornell and Harvard (the acronym stands for Salton's Magical Automated Retrieval Technique)(5). In this system, each document is represented by a set of concept numbers. A concept number represents keywords which have been reduced to a standard form by the control of synonyms and of word forms; for example, 648 might stand for the keywords catalog, catalogue, catalogs, cataloguing, recataloging and so on (this control is achieved partly by human effort, by the setting up of synonym dictionaries, for example, and partly automatically—eg through truncation). The set of concept numbers for a document is called a concept vector. When a request for documents on a subject is made, the request is presented to the computer as an enquiry vector—a set of keyword numbers produced in the same way as the concept vectors. The computer must then compare the enquiry vector against the concept vectors held in its memory, to select those which most nearly match.

Now, if the machine must match the enquiry vector against every concept vector in the memory, this may take,

124

in computer terms, a long time; and it may be an expensive process. The search time would be considerably reduced if the concept vectors were clustered—that is, classified—and each cluster given its own vector, so that the comparison could be made in two stages: first a comparison between the enquiry vector and each cluster vector, and then between the enquiry vector and each concept vector within the cluster which was selected at the first stage. Suppose that the collection contains 100 documents, each represented by its concept vector, and that these are not clustered; the computer must make 100 comparisons between the enquiry vector and the concept vectors in order to select those documents which will satisfy the enquiry. Now, suppose that the concept vectors have been clustered into ten groups, with an average of ten concept vectors in a cluster; the machine now has to perform only twenty comparisons to achieve the same result—ten against the cluster vectors, and, on average, ten against each concept vector in the selected cluster. In SMART, this clustering is achieved without human indexing effort: the documents—or rather their surrogates—are classified automatically.

Imagine that we have a collection consisting of five documents, and that these contain between them six 'concepts', which may be shown as concept numbers 001-006. If we assign the letters A-E to the documents we can construct the following matrix, in which 1 means that the document contains a given 'concept' and 0 means that it does not:

		Concept numbers					
		001	002	003	004	005	006
	A	0	1	0	1	1	0
	B	0	0	1	1	0	0
documents	C	1	0	1	0	0	1
	D	0	1	0	1	0	0
	E	1	0	0	0	1	1

We can now represent the concept vector for document A, for example, as 010110; and the computer can work out the strength of relationships between A and each other document, based on the proportion of shared concept numbers.

For example, documents A and B provide four concept numbers between them, and only one of these is shared by both documents; we can see that the strength of similarity may be shown as ¼, or 0.25. This figure is called the similarity coefficient. The similarity coefficients between A and each other document in the collection are:

A	B	C	D	E
1	0.25	0	0.66	0.20

In the same way, the computer can work out the similarity coefficients between every other pair of documents in the collection-

	A	B	C	D	E
B	0.25	1	0.25	0.33	0
C	0	0.25	1	0	0.50
D	0.66	0.33	0	1	0
E	0.20	0	0.50	0	1

At this stage we have the basis for the creation of five clusters —one which excludes document C (the group produced when similarities with A are measured); one which excludes E (the group based on B); one with A and D excluded (the group based on C); one with C and E excluded (the group based on D); and one with B and D excluded (the group based on E). Obviously, one of these clusters must be preferred—there is no point in having as many clusters as there are documents, because this would not reduce the search time. We would want that group which has the strongest relationships to be chosen; and, to ensure that this relatively strongly related group is absolutely worth creating, we would want it to satisfy two absolute conditions—that it should contain a minimum of N documents, and that their similarity coefficients with the document on which the group is based should be above a minimum of p. (If we do not impose these conditions we could have clusters created by the computer with insufficient documents to save search time, or with too weak relationships to satisfy the enquirer). In our unrealistic example of a collection consisting of five documents, we might impose the conditions that a cluster is only acceptable if it contains three or more documents with a similarity coefficient of at least 0.33. The only group to satisfy these conditions is that based on document D; if we now eliminate from that group documents with a similarity coefficient less than 0.33, we are left with a cluster composed of documents A, B and D, with D as the cluster centre. This cluster may be represented by a centroid vector (or classification vector) produced by the merging of the concept vectors for A, B and D.

The same process can be applied to documents left unclustered, and repeated until all, or most, are in a cluster, each cluster having its own centroid vector. At the search stage, the enquiry is reduced to a concept vector (called the enquiry vector), and this is first matched against the centroid vectors and then against each concept vector in the cluster selected by the first search as most closely matching the enquiry vector. The information about the documents in this cluster is then output in ranked order (that is, the document which most closely matches the enquiry vector is ranked 1, the second most closely matching is ranked 2, and so on); a cut-off point may be imposed, so that those documents whose similarity coefficient with the enquiry vector is too low are not presented to the enquirer.

Keyword classification
While SMART classifies document surrogates automatically, Karen Sparck Jones's keyword classification groups keywords automatically(6). The classification (or 'clumping') of keywords—that is, terms derived from the texts of documents and used as index terms—is thought to produce more efficient indexing than the use of simple keywords. The most obvious improvement is the increase in the number of documents produced by the system in response to an enquiry. Consider the following diagram (in which, as in all diagrams in this section, lower case letters on the left represent terms used by the searcher; lower case letters to the right represent keywords; numerals represent keyword classes; and upper case letters represent documents):

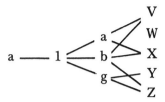

The enquirer has asked for documents containing the term (a). Without keyword classification the only documents retrieved by this term would be V and X; with it, documents W, Y and Z are also retrieved, because their keywords (b) and (g) form a clump with (a) in the keyword class 1. We can say that keyword classification has improved the recall of the system.

Keyword classification also improves precision—that is, a greater proportion of retrieved documents is useful to the enquirer. There are four ways of increasing precision through keyword classification: through context; through intersection; and through automatic weighting of keywords or of keyword classes. The following diagram illustrates context:

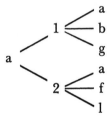

The keyword (a) appears in two different classes; if all the documents represented by these classes of keywords are retrieved, the enquirer will find many of them irrelevant. The relevant class of the two can be chosen by discovering what the other keywords are in each. For example, suppose that key word (a) is Alienation, (b) is Dropouts, (c) is Communes, (f) is Drama and (l) is Theatre; the enquirer looking for information on alienation as a social phenomenon can choose class 1, leaving class 2 to the enquirer who wants documents on alienation as a dramatist's technique.

Intersection occurs when the request includes more than one term, and they do not all appear in all of the relevant

128

keyword classes; for example, the search terms (a) and (f) in this diagram:

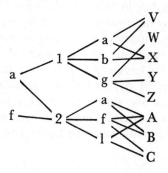

Here, it is obvious that the enquirer needs (a) in the sense it has when it appears in class 2—if we substitute the words given for the lower case letters in the previous paragraph we can see that he is interested in drama, not in sociology—and the computer will print out details of documents A, B and C only. We could be a little more sophisticated, and get the machine to display V, W, X, Y and Z as well, so as to increase recall, while ranking A, B and C above them, so as to diminish the loss of precision involved. This ranking could be achieved by weighting classes in proportion to the number of search terms they contain. Weighting could also be applied to keywords, allowing searches to be made under both keywords and keyword classes, while increasing precision.

All of these techniques depend on the classification of keywords, and this is achieved automatically. The basis for the grouping cannot be conventional semantic relationships, because the computer cannot know the meanings of words nor discover hierarchical relationships between them. Instead, Sparck Jones makes use of the concept of 'intersubstitutibility'—that two or more keywords may be equally good for retrieving the same subset of documents because they always occur together in the same document:

'A thesaurus classification ... consists of connected words which are intersubstitutible in retrieval. These words need not be synonyms or even near-synonyms, and they need not be generically related; for retrieval purposes, two words which are collocationally related, like "boundary" and "layer", may be acceptable substitutes for one another.'(7)

129

The technique used is similar to the clustering technique in SMART, in that similarity coefficients between each pair of things have to be computed; but in this case the things are keywords, and the similarity to be measured is the degree to which they co-occur. A simple formula for this coefficient is $N/(a + b) - N$, in which N represents the number of co-occurrences of keyword (a) with keyword (b), while a and b represent the total occurrences of each of these keywords. Four kinds of keyword classes are produced by this technique; they are called respectively strings, in which each keyword co-occurs significantly only with adjacent keywords:

$$a - b - c - d - e$$

stars, in which each keyword co-occurs with a common keyword:

```
    c
    |
b — a — d
    |
    e
```

cliques, in which each keyword co-occurs with every other:

```
a — b
|⨉|
c — d
```

and clumps, whose internal similarities are greater than those between their members and the keywords excluded from the clump:

It is fair to say that not all workers in this field agree that keyword classification does improve efficiency(8), but this need not concern us: our interest in it is as an attempt to classify things by computer, without human intellectual effort.

Book classification

An earlier use of the degree to which terms co-occur as the basis for automatic classification is the attempt to create a classification scheme and to classify books without intellectual indexing work reported by Borko and Bernick. This attempt was based on the assumption that 'documents can be classified on the basis of words they contain, and that documents containing similar sets of words belong to the same category.'(9)

Borko and his colleagues used 260 abstracts of computer literature to produce a classification of ninety previously selected terms. The keywords from the abstracts were fed into the computer, which worked out the number of times each of the ninety terms occurred in each of the documents, and, on this basis, the number of times each term co-occurred with each other term. Sets of co-occurring terms formed the classes—for example, the terms Average, Multiplication, Division, Equation constitute the class Arithmetic computation (the classes were named by humans, and groups of classes were also produced by humans rather than by the machine; but we need not worry about that). The terms were to act as 'clue words'; to indicate automatically the class to which a document containing them was to be assigned. The idea is simple enough, but there are two obvious complications. The first is that a term may be a clue word for more than one class (for example, the term Classification might, in such a system, be a clue word for Librarianship, but also for Zoology, Logic, Chemistry, Sociology etc); the second, that a document may contain terms which are clue words to different classes.

The first problem was solved by assigning a value to each clue word in each class, reflecting its reliability as an indicator that a document should be placed in that class. The basis for this 'factor loading' was the number of times the term co-occurred with the other clue words for the class in the original set of 260 abstracts. The solution to the second problem was to place the document in the class whose clue words achieved the highest score—the value of each clue word being the number of times it occurred in the document multiplied by its factor loading. Here is an example from

Borko and Bernick. Consider a document which contains the terms Analog (which occurs once), Coding (once), Conversion (twice) and Translation (once). These terms are clue words for five classes; which class should the document be placed in? The situation is shown in this matrix, which includes the factor loadings for the terms:

	Class 1 (Equations)	Class 8 (Code compression)	Class 14 (Analog computers)	Class 16 (Data transmission)	Class 21 (Mechanical translation)
Analog	.0773		.1363		
Coding		.2408		.1259	
Conversion		.1211(x2)			
Translation					.3325

We can see from the matrix that Translation, for example, is a clue word for class 21, Mechanical translation, with a factor loading of .3325; and that both Analog and Coding are ambiguous clue words, each leading to two classes (although we can also see for which of the two they are more reliable clue words—class 14 in the case of Analog, and class 8 in the case of Coding). The factor loading for Conversion in class 8 is to be multiplied by two because the term occurs twice in the document. If we now add up the score for each class it is clear that class 8 achieves the highest with .4830 (the sum of .2408 and .2422), and the document would be placed in that class.

Fortunately (see below) this technique produced poor results: when the 260 documents on which the classification was based were classified automatically, only 63.4% were correctly placed; and when a further 145 documents which had not been used in the construction of the system were classified, over 51% of them were incorrectly placed.

The three examples of automatic classification we have looked at merely illustrate the bases of the technique: many more attempts have been made, and will go on being made, with increasing sophistication—and perhaps increasing success. For the moment, automatic classification is not a threat to intellectual classification; we can still agree with Cuadra, who wrote ten years ago that 'the use of computer-generated classification schemes is not yet appropriate for most libraries or even for most semiautomated retrieval systems.'(10)

This is fortunate for those of us who believe that classification is a basic human intellectual activity (and whose jobs depend to some extent on it remaining so!) which should not be abandoned to the machine; but we must recognise that automatic classification does have a role in computerised information retrieval systems, and that the relationships it reveals are complementary to those which human classification is concerned with, and may help clients to achieve the lateral thinking which some critics of intellectually produced classifications claim they inhibit.

REFERENCES

1 Taube, Mortimer 'Functional approach to coordinate indexing' his *Studies in coordinate indexing* Documentation Inc, 1953.

2 Aitchison, Jean *Thesaurofacet* Whetstone, English Electric, 1969.

3 Richmond, Phyllis A 'The future of classification' *Drexel library quarterly* 10 (4) October 1974.

4 *Bath University comparative catalogue study: final report* BLRD, 1975.

5 Salton, Gerard *The SMART retrieval system* Englewood Cliffs, Prentice-Hall, 1971.

6 Jones, Karen Sparck, op cit.

7 Ibid.

8 Minker, J (et al) 'An evaluation of query expansion by the addition of clustered terms for a document retrieval system' *Information storage and retrieval*, 8 (6) 1972.

9 Borko, Harold and Bernick, Myrna 'Automatic document classification' *Journal of the Association for Computing Machinery* 10 (2) April 1963; reprinted in Saracevic, Tefko *Introduction to information science* New York London, Bowker, 1976.

10) Cuadra, Carlos A (et al) 'Technology and libraries' Knight, D M and Nourse, E S *Libraries at large* New York, London, Bowker, 1969.

INDEX

Usually only one form of a word is indexed, so that the form found in the index may not be that found in the text; this is particularly noticeable when the text word is changed so that it can stand alone in the index—for example, the term 'Modulate', found on page 55, is indexed as 'Modulation'. Homonyms are controlled (see 'Difference'), and all synonyms and near-synonyms used are separately indexed. In addition, if different synonyms are found on different text pages a *see also* reference is made between them in the index, thus:

Inclusion 21, 24, 41
sa Subordination

Subordination 17, 21, 76, 77
sa Inclusion

No proper names are indexed, except those of classification schemes.

Abstractions 9
Activities 9, 23
Addresses 72, 73, 74 *sa* Notation
Allocation 75, 76, 108
Alphabet (notation) 74, 79 *sa* Letters
Alphabetical order 40, 71
Alphabetical subject catalogues 14, 21
Alphabetical subject indexes 14, 47, 73, 101 ff
Alternative location 81 *sa* Flexibility

Analytico-synthetic schemes 28 *sa* Faceted schemes
Applications-with-science 112
Arbitrary symbols 74, 75, 81, 85, 95
Arithmetical notation 89
Arrays 37, 40, 41, 98
Aspect schemes 106 ff
Attributes facet 110
Author-attributed relationships 27 *sa* Complex classes
Automatic classification 123 ff

Autonomy of clients
14

Base (notation) 75, 88, 90,
91
Bias phase 20, 98, 99
Bibliographic classification
32, 35, 40, 74, 76, 77,
79, 81, 82, 84, 98, 106,
109, 112, 115, 116
Brevity 75, 77
Broader classes 41, 63, 78,
103, 105, 120 *sa* Super-
ordinate classes
Broader-narrower order 41,
43, 46, 59, 61, 66, 81, 82
Broader-narrower relationships 23, 24, 37, 55, 59,
119 *sa* Hierarchical relationships, Inclusion,
Subordination
Browsing 13, 14, 77

Canonical classes 98, 106
Canonical order 40
Catalogues 11, 13, 71,
119, 121
Centesimal notation 91
Centroid vectors 127
sa Cluster vectors
Chain 55, 90
Chain indexing 14, 103
Characteristics of division 9,
10, 18, 38, 41, 46, 52, 53,
57, 65
Chronological order 40 *sa*
Developmental order,
Evolutionary order
Citation order 37 ff, 42, 43,
54, 61, 62, 65, 66, 81, 82,
85 ff, 98, 99, 110, 119
Classes *passim*
Classes (in society) 10
Classification *passim*

Classification
definition 9
uses 10 ff
*Classification of library
information science* 73, 83,
84
Classification schemes *passim*
Classification schemes
definition 12, 13
Classification vectors 127
sa Cluster vectors
Classified catalogues 14, 73,
123
Cliques 130
Clue words 131, 132
Clumping 127, 128
Clumps 130
Cluster centre 127
Cluster vectors 125 *sa*
Centroid vectors
Clusters 125, 126, 127,
130
Collateral classes 25, 37,
41, 43, 47, 61, 65
Collection number 92
Collocation 13, 37, 38,
43, 47, 59, 61, 62, 71, 72,
73, 81, 106, 107, 111,
119
Collocationally related terms
129 *sa* Co-occurrence of
terms
Colon classification 33, 91,
98, 106, 109, 112
Common auxiliaries 116
Common facets 105, 115,
116
Comparison phase 19, 98
Complex classes 18, 19,
20, 27, 28, 98
Complexity (order in an
array) 40, 60
Composite classes 18, 19,
38, 71, 82

Compound classes 18, 19, 20, 27, 28, 30 ff, 41, 52, 83, 85, 98
Compound classes compared with superimposed 18, 49
Computers 28, 123, 124, 131 *sa* Automatic classification, Mechanised indexing
Concept indexing 12, 13, 124
Concept numbers 124, 126
Concept vectors 124, 125, 127
Concepts 10, 12, 13, 53, 59, 124 *sa* Ideas of things
Concrete schemes 109
Concreteness (order in an array) 39, 62, 66
Concretes 9, 109, 110
Consensus 39, 62, 66
Context (keyword classification) 128
Controlled vocabularies 13, 14, 123
Co-occurrence of terms 131 *sa* Collocationally related terms
Coordinate classes 25, 37, 40, 41, 46, 59, 78, 88, 90, 91, 106
Cross-classification 53
Cutter-Sanborn numbers 92
Decimal classification 27, 31, 32, 33, 34, 35, 36, 74, 75, 76, 77, 79, 88, 90, 103, 106, 107, 109, 111, 115, 116
Decimal notation 89 *sa* Divisible notation
Decimal principle 27
Decreasing concreteness 39, 62, 66
Definition (use of classification) 10

Dependence 39, 110, 112
Developmental order 40, 41, 65, 110 *sa* Chronological order, Evolutionary order
Difference (in definition) 10
Difference (phase relationship) 98
Directional phrase relationships 99
Disciplinary schemes 106 ff
Distributed relatives 38 *sa* Scattering
Divisible notation 89, 95
Document clustering 124 ff
Document number 93 *sa* Individualising symbols
Documents 11

Elemental classes 18, 19, 20, 27, 28, 30, 31, 32, 37, 38, 45, 46, 48, 49, 63, 71, 73, 80, 82, 88, 89
End product 39, 62 *sa* Purpose
Enquiry vectors 124, 125, 127
Entities 9, 106, 107, 109, 114
Entities facet 110
Enumerated classes 31, 35, 36, 53, 80, 83, 84, 88, 116
Enumeration 106, 115
Enumerative schemes 27, 28, 30, 31, 35, 37, 38, 41, 78, 88, 102
Enumerative schemes advantages 35
disadvantages 30 ff, 45
Evolutionary order 112, 114 *sa* Chronological order, Developmental order
Exhaustive division 55
Exposition phase 20

137

Expressive notation 77, 83 ff, 88, 95

Facet analysis 46 ff, 106, 110, 113
Facet indicators 82, 84, 85, 86, 88, 95
Faceted schemes 27, 28, 30, 32, 36, 37, 38, 61, 66, 73, 78, 83, 89, 102
Faceted schemes
  advantages 34
  construction 45 ff
  disadvantages 35
Facets 28, 45, 46, 47, 49, 52, 56, 57, 61, 65, 81, 82, 83, 84, 85, 87, 98, 110
Factor loading 131, 132
Fence 83, 84, 88, 95
Filing order 37, 40, 41, 47, 54, 59 ff, 71, 72, 74, 81, 82, 85, 86, 88, 98
Flexibility 81, 85, 88
Foci 45, 46, 47, 49, 53, 54, 55, 56, 57, 59, 65, 87
Form classes 116, 117
Forms of presentation 20, 35, 49, 98, 115, 116
Fractional notation 89
  Divisible notation
Fringe subjects 105
Fundamental categories 39

Gap notation 89
General citation order 39
General schemes 27, 35, 103 ff
General phase relationships 98
Generalia class 116
Generic relationships 22, 23, 27, 121, 129 sa Genus-species relationships
Generic structure 77, 83

Genus 10, 22, 53
Genus-species relationships 59, 60 sa Generic relationships
Gradation in speciality 112
Group notation 91

Helpful order 33, 34, 40, 71
Hierarchical notation 76 ff, 83, 90, 91, 95
Hierarchical relationships 17, 21, 22, 25, 27, 129 sa Broader-narrower relationships, Inclusion, Subordination
Hierarchies 10, 25, 38, 55, 56
Homonyms 12, 13, 48, 102
Hospitality 78, 88 ff

Ideas of things 9, 12 sa Concepts
In focus 45, 49
Inclusion 21, 24, 41 sa Broader-narrower relationships, Hierarchical relationships, Subordination
Increasing complexity 40
Increasing size 40, 60
Index vocabularies 13, 14
Indexes 12, 14, 47, 101 ff
Indexing 11, 12
Individualising symbols 92 sa Document number
Individuals 91
Influence phase 20, 98, 99
Integrative levels 114, 115
Interaction (in composite classes) 19
Intercalator 83 sa Fence
Interdisciplinary subjects 108

Intersection (keyword classi-
fication) 128
Intersubstitutibility 129
Inversion 43, 47, 54, 61, 63,
82, 83, 84, 87
Irrelevant documents 13, 17,
128
Isolates 46 *sa* Foci

Juxtaposition 13 *sa* Collocation

Keyword classification 119,
127 ff
Keyword-in-context 123
Keywords 124, 127, 129,
131 *sa* Natural language
vocabularies
KWOC 123

Lateral thinking 121, 133
Leap in division 55
Letters (notation) 74, 95
sa Alphabet
*Library of Congress classifi-
cation* 33, 35, 40, 74, 79,
89, 92, 109, 112
Literal mnemonics 79
Literature (as form class)
116
Logic 10
Logical division 53 ff, 56, 57
*London education classifi-
cation* 53, 54, 74, 80, 85, 89
Loose assemblages 19 *sa*
Author-attributed relation-
ships, Complex classes,
Phase relationships

Main classes 106 ff
Map of knowledge 10 *sa*
Structure of knowledge
Mechanised indexing 123 ff
sa Computers

Memorability 78, 79
Messages 11, 12
Mixed notation 74, 75, 84
Mnemonics 78, 79
Modulation 55
Mutually exclusive classes
53, 54
Names of things 12
Narrower-broader order
42, 43
Narrower classes 41, 42, 43,
103 *sa* Subordinate classes
Natural language vocabu-
laries 13 *sa* Keywords,
KWOC

Non-directional phase relationships 98
Non-hierarchical notation 77
sa Ordinal notation
Non-subject relationships
120
Notation 14, 27, 47, 61, 66,
71 ff, 106, 108, 110
Number-building *see* Synthesis
Numerals (notation) 74, 75

Objections to systematic
order 119 ff
One-place index 102
Open-access libraries 14
Operations 9, 23
Order in array 37, 40, 41,
46, 59, 60, 61, 65
Ordinal notation 77, 95

Parallel sequences 119
Partially comprehensive
classes 106
Parts 23
Pattern 10 *sa* Structure of
knowledge

Personality-Matter-Energy-
Space-Time 39
Pervasive subjects 116
Phase relationships 19, 20,
27, 98
Phases 19, 20, 98
Phenomena (in BC) 108
Physical form (of documents)
116
PMEST 39
Polytopical works 21, 49
Portmanteau classes 104
Post-coordinate indexes 14,
123
Precision 128, 129
Properties 9, 23
Pronounceable notation 79
sa Syllabic notation
Proximate division 55
Punched cards 78
Pure notation 74, 75, 84,
88
Purpose (in choice of citation
order) 39, 62, 66

Qualities (of things) 10

Recall 129
Reclassification 109
References 13, 14
Relationships between
classes 17 ff
Relative index 102, 103
Repeater digits 91
Research (use of classifica-
tion) 10
Retroactive notation 87, 88,
95

Scattering 37, 38, 102, 106,
107, 119
Schedules 66, 103
Sector notation 91

Semantic relationships 121,
129
Semantically non-obvious
relationships 121
Sequence notation 92
Shelf marks 72
Shelf order 14, 119
Similarity coefficients 126,
127, 130
Simple classes 18
Simplicity (notation) 75
Sioux Indians 10
Size (order in array) 40,
60
SMART 124 ff, 130
Spatial order 40, 59
Special auxiliaries 116
Special schemes 27, 35,
37, 105, 106
Species 22, 41, 53
Specific index 102
Specificity 17
Standard subdivisions 116
Stars 130
Strings 130
Structural notation 76, 77,
83
Structure of knowledge 105,
106, 108, 121 sa Map
of knowledge
Structured vocabularies 13,
14, 124
Study (use of classification)
10
Subfacets 46, 47, 52 ff,
59 ff, 81, 82, 84
Subject classification 109,
112, 116
Subject indexes 14, 47
Subordinate classes 25, 41,
59, 76, 77, 83, 88, 89, 90
sa Narrower classes
Subordination 17, 21, 76,
77 sa Broader-narrower

Subordination *(continued)*
relationships, Hierarchical
relationships, Inclusion
Subsets 11, 12
Suggestive mnemonics 80
Superimposed classes 18 ff,
27, 28, 30, 31, 38, 41, 49,
52, 53, 57, 61, 62, 71, 82,
98
Superimposed classes com-
pared with compound 18,
49
Supermarkets (use of classification) 11
Superordinate classes 25, 41,
55, 56, 78, 90, 102, 120
sa Broader classes
Synonyms 12, 13, 48, 101,
102, 104, 124, 129
Syntactical relationships
17, 18, 83
Syntactical structure (expressive notation) 77
Synthesis 27, 30, 32, 35, 36,
78, 80, 83, 84, 85, 87, 88,
115, 116

Systematic mnemonics 78
Systematic order 12, 13,
14, 47, 71, 119, 121,
123
Systematic schedules 116

Thesauri 14
Thought (use of classifica-
tion) 10
Truncation 124

Unique notation 82
Uniquely defining class 108
*Universal decimal classifi-
cation* 74, 76, 78, 85, 90,
91, 108, 109, 111, 116
Unnamed concepts 12

Wall-picture principle 39
sa Dependence
Weighting 128, 129
Word forms 124